mastering the art of
sous vide
cooking

Unlock the Versatility of Precision Temperature Cooking

justice stewart
founder of Gourmet De–Constructed

PAGE STREET
PUBLISHING CO.

PAGE STREET
PUBLISHING CO.

First published in 2018 by
Page Street Publishing Co.
27 Congress Street, Suite 105
Salem, MA 01970
www.pagestreetpublishing.com

Distributed by Macmillan, sales in Canada by The Canadian Manda Group.

22   21   20   19   3   4   5

ISBN-13: 978-1-62414-666-4
ISBN-10: 1-62414-666-X

Library of Congress Control Number: 2018956363

Cover and book design by Laura Gallant for Page Street Publishing Co.
Photography by Cheyenne Cohen and Mandy Maxwell
Image on page 187 (bottom right) © Shutterstock/Oleg Troino

Printed and bound in the United States

This book is dedicated to the trio of women who raised me:

Grandma Janie; my mom, Barbara; and my Aunt Doris.

contents

Foreword by V. Sheree Williams   6

Introduction   7

Sous Vide Basics   11

Chapter 1
Breathtaking Beef   15
Memphis-Style Barbecue Bleu Cheese Burgers   17

Texas-Style Espresso-Rubbed Porterhouse   18

Argentine Skirt Steak with Chimichurri   21

Chacarero: Chilean Beef Sandwich   22

Jamaican Oxtail Stew   25

Florentine Steak   26

Guinness Corned Beef   29

Chateaubriand with Red Wine Sauce   30

Southeast Asian–Style Spicy Short Ribs   33

Beef Ramen   34

Veal Oscar   37

Veal Roulades with Juniper Butter   38

Veal Pastrami   41

Chapter 2
Foolproof Poultry & Fowl   43
Blackened Chicken Maque Choux   45

Italian-Style Grilled Chicken Sandwich   46

Garlicky Chicken Thighs   49

Madras Curry Chicken   50

Spinach and Sundried Tomato–Stuffed
Chicken Rolls   53

Chicken Shawarma with Pistachio Yogurt   54

Djaj Bil-Bahar Il-Asfar (Persian Spiced Chicken)   57

Cambodian-Style Chicken Salad   58

Pan-Seared Duck Breast with Pomegranate Dressing   61

Duck Leg Confit   62

Sriracha-Glazed Duck with Pineapple Salsa   65

Chapter 3
Perfectly Poached Pork   67
Feijoada (Portuguese Stew)   69

Pernil   70

Miami Cubano Sandwich   73

Iberico Pork Tenderloin with Cherry–Mustard Sauce   74

Sausage and Peppers   77

Sweet and Spicy Soy-Glazed Pork Chops   78

Lemongrass Pork Ribs   81

"Roasted" Pork Belly   82

Pork Cutlets with Marsala Wine and Wild Mushrooms   85

Chapter 4
Luscious Lamb   87
Cumin-Spiced Lamb Burger   89

Lamb Necks with Saffron Couscous   90

Grilled Leg of Lamb with Gjetost Sauce   93

Rack of Lamb with Butter and Garlic Asparagus   94

Grilled Lamb Chops with Tomato–Prune Sauce   97

Lamb Shanks with Garlic Mashed Potatoes   98

Chapter 5

Superb Seafood   101

Lobster Fettuccine in Herbed Cream Sauce   103

Pacific Salmon with Citrus Kale Salad   104

Mediterranean Octopus Salad   107

Monkfish with Saffron Beurre Blanc   108

Dill Salmon   111

Drunken Rose Red Snapper   112

Scallops à l'Américaine   115

Goan Shrimp   116

Sea Bass in Tuscan Kale   119

Chapter 6

Sensational Small Plates & Starters   121

Moroccan-Style Sticky Meatballs   123

Gyro Sliders with Tzatziki   124

Classic Lobster Rolls   127

Veal Tongue Tacos   128

Sichuan Surf & Turf Meatballs   131

Pulpo Gallego   132

Fiery Harissa Shrimp   135

Gochujang Cold Squid   136

Chapter 7

Beautiful Brunches   139

Crab Cakes with Poached Eggs and Saffron Hollandaise   141

Mexican Brunch Burger   142

Crustless Quiche Lorraine   145

Hawaiian Loco Moco   146

Chapter 8

Vivid Vegetable Sides   149

Honey-Glazed Heirloom Carrots   151

Vinegar and Herb Potato Salad   152

Butter and Garlic Asparagus   155

Caramelized Cabbage Wedges   156

Buttery Root Vegetables   159

Garlic Mashed Potatoes   160

Chapter 9

Delectable Desserts   163

Cardamom-Spiced Pears in Red Wine   165

Berry Cheesecake   166

Nutty Crème Brûlée   169

Banana Pudding Pie with Rum-Infused Whipped Cream   170

Chapter 10

Classic Condiments   173

Saffron Hollandaise   175

Béarnaise Sauce   176

Pickled Red Onions   179

Dill Pickles   180

Dulce de Leche   183

Essential Equipment   185

Acknowledgments   188

About the Author   189

Index   190

foreword

Over the last eight years, I have had the honor of meeting and writing about so many amazing chefs from around the world and from all walks of life. When I met Justice Stewart and learned more about his story, I knew he would one day have the opportunity to share his love of cooking with the world.

I am one of those home cooks who is still learning and searching for techniques and recipes that fit my interest and lifestyle. When Justice told me that he was writing a cookbook about sous vide, I became very excited and I know followers of his popular blog, Gourmet De-Constructed, will be too.

Mastering the Art of Sous Vide Cooking is right on time as chefs and home cooks talk about bringing sous vide into the kitchen. Similar to pressure cooking, it is one of those cooking methods that is being rediscovered, and Justice does a great job introducing this method as well as creating recipes that allow you to start slow with simple dishes as you build your confidence to experiment with some of the more complex ones.

If you are new to sous vide cooking, don't worry, as this book will walk you through the basics and get you prepared to create recipes that will burst with flavor. If you have sous vide cooking skills up your sleeve, get ready to unleash even more creativity.

It is hard to live in New York and not be influenced by the melting pot of cultures. What I love most about Justice is the way he cooks outside of the box, experimenting with ingredients and dishes that speak to who he is as a curious chef and true New Yorker. Just as he does every time he steps into the kitchen, I encourage you to keep an open mind as he takes you on a culinary adventure around the world; all through the art of sous vide.

Through his guidance and ease, Justice shows you that nothing is off limits when it comes to using this method. From stews, burgers, sandwiches, vegetable sides and even condiments and desserts, get ready to cook like you have never done before.

As you begin to turn the pages and try the recipes that follow, be prepared to deconstruct the way you think about cooking and at the same time fall in love with it all over again.

—V. Sheree Williams, Publisher and Editor-in-Chief, *Cuisine Noir* magazine

introduction

The science of sous vide cooking was discovered in a sort of accidental way by a physicist named Benjamin Thompson in 1799. As the story is told, he tried roasting a mutton shoulder in a device he created to dry potatoes with hot air currents. After three hours he gave up and handed the task over to the household maids who left the mutton in the machine overnight. The next day he discovered a perfectly cooked mutton shoulder that had maintained its flavor and juiciness. He was quoted as saying of the results, "Not merely eatable, but perfectly done, and most singularly well-tasted."

I discovered the sous vide method many years ago as a professional chef—the sous vide machine has been around since the 1970s, after all. But back then it was only utilized by high-end restaurants due to its size and price. With advances in technology over the last twenty years, the device has gotten much smaller, more affordable and easier for the home cook to use. I am thrilled to let you in on this industry secret because it has been an invaluable piece of equipment in my kitchen for years.

I was born in Queens, New York, and raised in Ravenswood Housing projects. My father passed away when I was ten years old, but I still hold on to very fond memories of him. He and I both loved fishing. We often went on group fishing trips in the Rockaways or Sheepshead Bay, Brooklyn. When it was time to cook our catch, my grandmother and aunt would take charge and not allow anyone else in their kitchen; my mom was not a big fan of cooking but she occasionally would jump in and help out, along with my sisters. The aromas of deep-fried, freshly caught fish along with other contemporary soul food would permeate our home and the immediate neighborhood, which sometimes enticed passersby to drop in for a plate. These are some of the best memories that I have of my family spending time together celebrating food.

As I got older, I began cooking a whole lot more in my off time. I would come home from a back-breaking day in construction and experiment with different recipes and ingredients. I never understood people who found cooking to be a chore; it was a relaxing evening and weekend hobby for me. I would read dozens of cookbooks and watch instructional culinary videos in my spare time. Soon, I began hosting and cooking small dinner parties for family and friends. People would tell me how amazing my food tasted, and they would always ask why I wasn't already in the restaurant industry.

Encouraged, I started my food blog, Gourmet De-Constructed, so that I could share my passion with the world. Then one day a chef from Louisiana with a catering business here in New York approached me and asked if I would like to cook for his company and, after some natural nervousness, I accepted. We prepared food for a major social media company based in Manhattan, and I really gained some valuable skills as far as cooking in a professional setting. I moved on after a period of time, and I eventually cooked my way into Madison Square Garden (MSG) as a sous chef in a Jean-Georges Vongerichten kitchen for the VIP clientele and season ticket holders during the

New York Knicks and Rangers home games. It was here that I gained the vast knowledge of cooking for hundreds of clients at once—often relying on the sous vide method.

During my time at MSG, I took charge of all of the sous vide cooking and learned so much more about utilizing this style of cooking. I eventually left MSG and started my own catering business, but I often still rely on the sous vide method.

I've learned a lot over the years and I am compelled to share what I've learned with others. I've been lucky enough to put myself in a position to help at-risk youth that were like me by sharing my story, and I return to my old neighborhood as often as I can to speak at schools or cook for charity events. Now, here, with this book, I want to share my knowledge with everyday cooks so they can take their sous vide meal preparation to the next level.

How many times have you cooked your expensive filet mignon into oblivion? It will never happen again with sous vide cooking. During the normal process of high-temperature cooking, certain nutrients in food are damaged and lost. Utilizing the sous vide method of cooking, the breakdown of nutrient is minimized while the overall flavor of your food is enhanced. That means you can cook your meat to the perfect temperature without the guesswork so you get fantastic flavor and texture every time.

And I don't mean just beef! Most sous vide beginners tend to only prepare their favorite steak with this style of cooking, but sous vide is much more versatile than that. Pork, beef, seafood, poultry and vegetables all do well and remain flavorful and juicy when cooked with this method. Delicious desserts can also be added to your water bath repertoire! You can also walk away from some of your foods during sous vide cooking, which you would never do while utilizing many traditional methods, so it can free you up to prepare other items on your menu, or just relax.

In these pages, you will learn how easy and versatile cooking with a sous vide device can be. You will take a culinary journey around the world as I introduce simple and easy-to-follow recipes and help build your skills to tackle the more complex dishes. Be prepared to impress your friends and family at that next dinner party—with these amazing recipes cooked with your very own electronic "sous chef," you can't lose!

sous vide basics

Food Safety

You've probably heard that in order for chicken to be safe, it ought to be cooked all the way to 165°F (74°C). This is not the case with the sous vide method in which you can cook the chicken to as low as 149°F (65°C). Traditional methods of cooking destroy bacteria and other microorganisms with high heat. The protein is brought to a temperature high enough to kill these germs quickly and it has worked for humans for eons. With the sous vide method, some food items are often cooked in the "danger zone" for microorganisms to grow (40°F [4°C] to 140°F [60°C]). But, don't worry! Here, the science of pasteurization (the same process that makes milk safe to drink) takes over and the longer cook times combine with lower temperatures to destroy any microorganisms in a process called low-temperature-long-time treatment (LTLT). This process uses lower heat for a longer time to kill pathogenic bacteria. So rest assured, as long as you keep a clean cooking environment and follow the proper cooking times, you will avoid becoming sick.

Important Note: I do not recommend cooking your food items in the sous vide bath for more than 72 hours, as bacteria, such as botulism, may occur.

Water Displacement Method

For cooks who do not own a vacuum-sealing machine, using this procedure is essential for cooking with the sous vide method. The process involves placing your item into a ziplock freezer bag and slowly submerging it into the water bath, while allowing all of the air to escape from the top of the bag. The bag is then sealed, and a kitchen clip is used to secure it to the cooking vessel. These bags can be used for almost all of the recipes in this book.

Important Note: I do not recommend using freezer bags for any recipe that calls for a temperature over 160°F (71°C). This type of bag tends to become compromised and will fail at the seams when cooked at high temperatures, especially over extended periods of time.

Mason/Canning Jars

When cooking with canning jars, screw the cap on completely tight and then slightly loosen it so the jar is not closed airtight, which can cause it to crack during cooking. Doing this allows the gas that builds inside the jar to escape slowly, without allowing water into the jar.

Some Additional Tips

Aromatics such as fresh herbs can be added to the bag to enhance the aroma and flavor of your foods. I find that fresh herbs sometimes become rancid over an extended cooking time, so I prefer to use a small amount of dried herbs, dried garlic and dried onion. Dry spices can be very strong, so when using them, go lightly, or you risk over-powering the flavor of the food item. Adding butter or olive oil is also optional. Sous vide cooking keeps the food flavorful, so you can just add salt and pepper and still end up with amazing results.

When cooking sous vide, especially at higher temperatures, the water will slowly evaporate. Keep an eye on it and occasionally add hot water when necessary.

General Cooking Times

These basic cooking times should help you get started on your sous vide adventure. Note that pork should be cooked from medium rare to well done, and chicken should always be prepared well done.

Beef, Veal and Lamb	Rare	Medium Rare	Medium Well	Well Done
Beef Steaks, Veal Chops or Lamb Chops (bone in, 1 to 2 inches [2.5 to 5 cm] thick)	125°F (51.6°C) 2 hours	134°F (56.6°C) 2 to 4 hours	145°F (62.7°C) 2 to 4 hours	156°F (69°C) 2 to 4 hours
Beef Tenderloin	125°F (51.6°C) 1 to 4 hours	130°F (54.4°C) to 134°F (56.6°C) 1 to 4 hours	140°F (60°C) 2 to 4 hours	156°F (69°C) 2 to 4 hours
Beef Roast	125°F (51.6°C) 7 to 12 hours	134°F (56.6°C) 24 hours	140°F (60°C) 12 to 24 hours	158°F (70°C) 6 to 10 hours
Leg of Lamb (boneless)	124°F (51°C) 3 to 6 hours	134°F (56.6°C) 4 to 6 hours	150°F (65.5°C) 4 to 6 hours	155°F (68.3°C) 4 to 6 hours

Pork	Medium Rare	Medium Well	Well Done
Pork Chops (bone in)	140°F (60°C) 2 to 4 hours	144°F (62°C) 2 to 4 hours	160°F (71°C) 2 to 4 hours
Pork Tenderloin	130°F (54.4°C) 2 to 4 hours	150°F (65.5°C) 2 to 4 hours	160°F (71°C) 2 to 4 hours
Pork Ribs	145°F (62.7°C) 24 hours	154°F (68°C) 24 hours	165°F (73.8°C) 12 hours

Poultry	Medium Rare	Well Done
Chicken Breast	-----	145°F (62.7°C) to 150°F (65.5°C) 2 hours
Chicken Thighs	-----	165°F (73.8°C) 2 to 4 hours
Duck Breast	134°F (56.6°C) 2 to 4 hours	-----
Duck Leg	155°F (68.3°C) 24 to 36 hours	-----

Seafood	Lower Temperature/More Tender	Higher Temperature/More Firm
Fish	Lightly flaky and firm: 122°F (50°C) 35 minutes to 1 hour	Moderately flaky and firm: 131°F (55°C) 35 minutes to 1 hour
Lobster	Tender and juicy: 131°F (55.5°C) 1 hour	Juicy and firm: 140°F (60°C) 30 to 45 minutes
Shrimp	Moist, juicy and tender: 135°F (57°C) 30 minutes to 1 hour	Traditional texture and juicy: 140°F (60°C) 30 minutes to 1 hour
Scallops	123°F (50.5°C) 30 minutes	Not recommended. Scallops tend to easily become rubbery at higher temperatures
Octopus	171°F (77.2°C) 6 hours	Not recommended.

Type of Vegetable	Standard Temperature/Time
Root Vegetables (e.g., carrots, rutabagas, parsnips, potatoes)	185°F (85°C) 2 to 4 hours
Green Vegetables (e.g., asparagus, green beans)	180°F (82.2°C) 10 to 15 minutes

breathtaking beef

Beef is one of the most commonly consumed meats in the world, and for good reason. From the humble ground beef burger to the elegant (read: expensive) chateaubriand, there is a beef-based entrée for everybody. While steak is the most commonly prepared cut of beef cooked in a sous vide bath, there are other cuts that do wonderfully in the temperature-controlled water bath. The tougher cuts require longer cook times, but the rewards are worth your efforts and patience.

Memphis-Style Barbecue Bleu Cheese Burgers

Memphis is a music town famous for blues and BBQ feasts. These burgers are big on both BBQ and blues (bleu cheese that is).

Serves: 4

Sous vide cook time: 1 hour

Preheat the water bath to 134°F (56.6°C). In a large salad bowl, whisk the mayonnaise, sugar, vinegar, lemon juice and celery seeds until fully incorporated. Stir in the tomato, green onion, bleu cheese crumbles and coleslaw. Season with salt and pepper, then refrigerate for at least 1 hour.

Place the beef in a mixing bowl with the salt, pepper, garlic powder, onion powder and BBQ sauce and gently knead the mixture with your hands until combined. Form 4 flat patties with the beef with 1 ounce (28 g) of bleu cheese in the center of each. Fold the sides of the meat up and over the cheese and reshape into patties. Place the burgers in a single layer in a bag and vacuum seal it, then place into the water bath. Cook for 1 hour.

Heat the oil in a skillet over medium-high heat. Remove the burgers from the bags and pat dry with paper towels. When the pan is hot, sear the burgers on each side until browned. Place the burgers on toasted buns and top them with the tomato slaw and crumbled bacon.

Tomato Slaw

1¼ cups (275 g) mayonnaise

2 tbsp (24 g) granulated sugar

1½ tbsp (22 ml) white wine vinegar

1 tsp lemon juice

½ tsp celery seeds

½ cup (90 g) diced tomato

2 tbsp (12 g) chopped green onion

2 oz (56 g) bleu cheese crumbles

16 oz (455 g) store-bought coleslaw

Kosher salt

Black pepper

Burgers

2 lbs (910 g) ground beef, 20% fat

Kosher salt

Black pepper

1 tsp garlic powder

1 tsp onion powder

4 oz (120 ml) BBQ sauce

4 oz (115 g) bleu cheese, divided

2 tbsp (30 ml) grapeseed oil

4 hamburger buns, toasted

¼ cup (80 g) bacon crumbles, from about 4 slices

Texas-Style Espresso-Rubbed Porterhouse

Nothing says Texas like a big ol' slab of bone-in steak. This porterhouse for two is cooked at a controlled temperature, which results in a perfectly cooked steak every time.

Serves: 2

Sous vide cook time: 4 hours

Preheat the water bath to 134°F (56.6°C). Whisk together the espresso, brown sugar, garlic powder, onion powder, cayenne, paprika, chili powder, salt and pepper in a medium bowl until they are completely incorporated. Season the steak generously with the rub on all sides and place it in a vacuum bag with the fresh thyme. Cook for 4 hours.

Remove the steak from the water and bag and pat dry with paper towels. Sprinkle the steak with more espresso rub, if desired. Add the grapeseed oil to a frying pan and place over high heat. When the oil begins to smoke, sear the steak on all sides to achieve your preferred level of char. Allow the steaks to rest off the heat for 10 minutes before slicing and serving. This steak pairs really well with Vinegar and Herb Potato Salad (page 152) and Butter and Garlic Asparagus (page 155).

> **Note:** The remaining seasoning mix can be sealed in an airtight container and stored in a dry cool place for up to 6 months.

¼ cup (22 g) espresso, such as Café Bustelo

¼ cup (55 g) brown sugar

1 tbsp (10 g) garlic powder

1 tbsp (7 g) onion powder

2 tsp (4 g) cayenne pepper

1 tbsp (7 g) paprika

2 tbsp (14 g) ancho chili powder

2 tbsp (17 g) kosher salt

1 tbsp (7 g) black pepper

1 (2-lb [910-g]) or 2 (1-lb [455-g]) porterhouse steak(s)

2 sprigs fresh thyme

2 tbsp (30 ml) grapeseed oil

Argentine Skirt Steak with Chimichurri

When I think of Argentina I think of gauchos and, of course, beef. This delicious skirt steak comes out fork tender and is served with a garlic, parsley and oregano sauce.

Serves: 4 to 6
Sous vide cook time: 3 hours 10 minutes

In a food processor, blend the balsamic vinegar, oil, Worcestershire, garlic, shallots, cayenne, cilantro, salt and pepper until smooth. Put the steak in a large bowl and pour the mixture on top, turning to completely coat the steak. Cover and refrigerate for 4 to 6 hours.

Clean the processor and add the parsley, olive oil, red wine vinegar, garlic, oregano, cumin and salt. Blend until smooth, taste and adjust seasoning if necessary, then stir in the pepper flakes. Set aside at room temperature until the steak is finished.

Preheat the water bath to 134°F (56.6°C). Remove the steak from the bowl, wipe off any excess marinade, place in a bag and vacuum seal it. Cook for 3 hours. Oil the grates of a grill and set the flame to high. When the grill is smoking hot, place the steak on it and cook 3 minutes per side, then allow it to rest on a plate for 5 to 10 minutes. Serve thinly sliced, drizzled with the chimichurri sauce.

Steak

¼ cup (60 ml) balsamic vinegar

½ cup (120 ml) grapeseed or canola oil

¼ cup (60 ml) Worcestershire sauce

2 cloves garlic, chopped

2 small shallots, roughly chopped

1 tsp cayenne pepper

¼ cup (8 g) chopped fresh cilantro leaves

1 tbsp (8 g) kosher salt

1 tsp freshly ground black pepper

3 lbs (1.4 kg) skirt steak, cleaned of all exterior fat and connective tissue

Chimichurri Sauce

1¼ cups (75 g) fresh Italian parsley, packed tight

½ cup (120 ml) olive oil

¼ cup (60 ml) red wine vinegar

4–5 cloves garlic, roughly chopped

1 tbsp (3 g) fresh oregano, finely chopped

½ tsp ground cumin

½ tsp kosher salt

1 tsp dried red pepper flakes

Chacarero: Chilean Beef Sandwich

Simple and delicious, this Chilean sandwich can be made with either thinly sliced steak or stewed pork on a roll with tomatoes, green beans and chili peppers. This version features tender sirloin, cooked to slow perfection in a water bath.

Serves: 4

Sous vide cook time: 3 hours

Preheat the water bath to 134°F (56.6°C). Put the garlic and onion flakes into a bag. Season the steak with salt and pepper, then place in the bag, vacuum seal it and cook for 3 hours.

In a bowl, mash the avocado with the lime juice and a pinch of salt, then cover and refrigerate.

Bring a pot of water to a boil and add the green beans. Cook for 4 to 5 minutes until they are slightly soft, then drain and run the beans under cold water until they are cooled off. Set aside.

Remove the steak from the bag and pat dry with paper towels. Heat a grill to high, if you are using one, and oil the grates. When the grill is smoking hot, sear each side of the steak until browned, 3 to 4 minutes per side. If you are using a pan, heat the oil over high heat and brown both sides of the steak. Using a kitchen torch with a Searzall® attachment eliminates the need for the oil. Simply run the flame along the steak, keeping the fire at least 4 inches (10 cm) off the meat until all sides are browned.

With a sharp knife, cut the steak crosswise (against the grain) into thin strips. Set the toasted Kaiser rolls on a counter and spread some avocado onto the top of each bun and add one slice of cheese to the bottom half. Add equal amounts of steak strips to each bun, then top with the green beans, sliced tomato and banana pepper rings and serve with hot sauce, if using.

1 tbsp (10 g) dried garlic flakes

1 tbsp (7 g) dried onion flakes

1 (1½-lb [680-g]) sirloin steak

½ tsp kosher salt

½ tsp black pepper

2 avocados, peeled and pitted

2 tbsp (30 ml) lime juice

12 oz (340 g) fresh green beans, trimmed and cut on a sharp bias into long, thin strips

2 tbsp (30 ml) grapeseed oil

4 Kaiser rolls, toasted

4 slices Muenster cheese

1 large tomato, sliced

2 pickled banana peppers, thinly sliced

Hot sauce, optional

Jamaican Oxtail Stew

I've always considered myself lucky to be living around so much authentic Jamaican food in Brooklyn, New York. Savory, sticky and spiced, this curry oxtail is at home in the city or the islands.

Serves: 4 to 6

Sous vide cook time: 24 hours

Preheat the water bath to 180°F (82.2°C). Season the beef with salt, pepper and 1½ tablespoons (10 g) of the curry powder. Heat 2 tablespoons (30 ml) of the oil in a large sauté pan over high heat and brown the oxtails, about 2 to 3 minutes per side, and place on a plate.

Heat the remaining 2 tablespoons (30 ml) of the oil in the same pan and add the onion, bell pepper and Scotch bonnet peppers. Sauté the vegetables, stirring occasionally, until they are softened, about 8 to 10 minutes. Season the mixture with the remaining 1½ tablespoons (10 g) of the curry powder, then add the garlic and cook until fragrant, about 45 seconds. Stir in the beef stock while scraping up any brown bits from the bottom of the pan and simmer until the liquid reduces to 2 cups (480 ml), about 10 to 15 minutes. Remove the pan from the heat and allow it to cool for 10 to 15 minutes. Place the browned oxtail in a vacuum bag, pour the reserved liquid into it and seal. Place the bag into the sous vide bath and cook for 24 hours.

After 24 hours, carefully remove the bag from the water (see Note) and pour the contents into a large saucepan over medium-high heat. Stir in the butter beans and allow them to warm, about 5 to 10 minutes, then serve with white rice.

Notes: Be sure to use gloves when handling the notoriously hot Scotch bonnet pepper and keep your hands away from your face after handling.

At such high temperatures, vacuum bags can become very soft and their structural integrity can become compromised. You will want to consider how to remove the bag safely from scalding water. Try using tongs to retrieve the bag and having a pot ready for immediate transfer.

2 lbs (910 g) beef oxtail, cut into 2-inch (5-cm) pieces

Kosher salt

Black pepper

3 tbsp (20 g) Jamaican curry powder, divided

¼ cup (60 ml) grapeseed oil, divided

1 large onion, finely chopped

1 large red bell pepper, finely chopped

2 Scotch bonnet peppers, finely chopped

3 cloves garlic, minced

3 cups (720 ml) beef stock

1 (15.5-oz [440-g]) can butter beans

White rice, for serving

Florentine Steak

Florentine steak is an Italian-style rosemary-flavored steak. Cooking it in the sous vide will significantly enhance the aromas and flavors of this dish. Use this method when cooking your T-bone and instantly elevate your next steak dinner at home. This dish is traditionally served with cannellini beans and lemon wedges.

Serves: 2
Sous vide cook time: 4 hours

Preheat the water bath to 134°F (56.6°C). Season the steaks with salt and pepper. Place the steaks into two separate bags and in each bag add 2 sprigs of rosemary, 1 tablespoon (10 g) of garlic flakes and 1 tablespoon (15 ml) of olive oil. Vacuum seal the bags and place into the sous vide bath for 4 hours.

Remove the steaks from the bags and pat dry with paper towels. Heat the grapeseed oil in a pan over medium-high heat until it is smoking. Sear the steaks until browned, about 2 to 3 minutes per side. Optionally, you can use a kitchen torch with the Searzall attachment to give the steak a charbroiled flavor. Serve with lemon wedges.

2 (16-oz [455-g]) T-bone steaks

Kosher salt

Black pepper

4 sprigs rosemary

2 tbsp (20 g) dried garlic flakes

2 tbsp (30 ml) olive oil

2 tbsp (30 ml) grapeseed oil

Lemon wedges, for serving

Guinness Corned Beef

Nothing reminds me more of the Emerald Isle than Guinness stout, which flavors this beloved Irish-American celebratory dish. The stout adds a light sweetness to the fatty flavors of the cured beef and the cooking method will make this brisket a new family favorite beyond St. Patrick's Day!

Serves: 8 to 10

Sous vide cook time: 48 hours

Preheat the water bath to 140°F (60°C). Rub the pickling spice on the surface of the brisket on all sides. Place the meat into a vacuum bag with the bay leaf, beef stock and Guinness stout and vacuum seal. Place it in the water bath and cook for 48 hours. Check the water level occasionally and add warm water as needed.

Remove the beef from the water bath and allow it to cool, about 15 minutes. Cut open the bag and remove the beef to a cutting board. Slice and serve with mustard, cabbage, carrots and potatoes (if using).

2 tbsp (12 g) pickling spice (if a spice packet is not included with the corned beef)

6 lbs (2.7 kg) corned beef brisket

1 bay leaf

½ cup (120 ml) beef stock

6 oz (177 ml) Guinness stout

Grain mustard, for serving

Caramelized Cabbage Wedges (page 156), for serving

Honey-Glazed Heirloom Carrots (page 151), for serving

Boiled potatoes, for serving, optional

Chateaubriand with Red Wine Sauce

Leaner cuts of beef like tenderloin benefit from the controlled temperature environment of the sous vide, allowing the more delicate beef flavor to develop. This perfectly cooked center cut of beef tenderloin makes for an impressive holiday showpiece, especially when it is sliced tableside and served with a classic, full-bodied French red wine sauce.

Serves: 6

Sous vide cook time: 3 hours

Tie the tenderloin at ½-inch (13-mm) intervals with kitchen twine and refrigerate it for at least 3 hours before pre-searing the beef (see Note).

Preheat the water bath to 134°F (56.6°C). Season the beef with salt and pepper. Heat 2 tablespoons (30 ml) of oil in a large skillet over high heat and quickly brown the tenderloin, 3 minutes per side. Remove it from the pan and set it aside. Add the thyme, rosemary and garlic to the pan and toast lightly, about 1 to 2 minutes, then place the sauce into a vacuum bag. Add the tenderloin to the bag and vacuum seal, then put it into the sous vide bath for 3 hours.

While the beef cooks, in a small bowl mash the flour and butter together with a fork, then set it aside.

In a saucepan over medium-high heat, add the chicken stock, beef stock and the bottle of wine. Bring to a boil, lower the heat to medium and cook the mixture, stirring occasionally, until it reduces to about 2 cups (480 ml), about 45 minutes. Remove the pan from the heat, cover and set it aside.

Remove the tenderloin from the sous vide bath and strain any remaining liquid into the saucepan with the wine mixture. Pat the beef dry with paper towels and season with salt and pepper. Heat the remaining 2 tablespoons (30 ml) of oil in the skillet until it is smoking hot, then sear the beef until a nice crust forms, 3 minutes per side. Remove the beef from the pan and plate it under tented foil.

Add the shallots to the pan and sauté them until they are soft and translucent, about 6 to 7 minutes, then add the garlic and cook for 2 minutes until fragrant. Deglaze the pan with the wine mixture, scraping up any browned bits. Bring the wine mixture to a boil and whisk in the butter and flour mixture until the sauce becomes smooth. Simmer until the mixture thickens and coats the back of a spoon, 5 to 12 minutes. Stir in the parsley and remove from the heat. Taste for seasoning and add more salt and pepper if desired. Slice the roast and serve drizzled with the wine sauce.

Note: Refrigerating the tenderloin ahead of pre-searing will chill the center of the beef and prevent it from cooking beyond the surface of the meat.

2 lbs (910 g) center-cut beef tenderloin

Kosher salt

Black pepper

¼ cup (60 ml) olive oil, divided

2 sprigs fresh thyme

2 sprigs rosemary

1 clove garlic, crushed

Red Wine Sauce

1 tbsp (8 g) all-purpose flour

2 tbsp (28 g) unsalted butter, softened to room temperature

3½ cups (830 ml) low sodium chicken stock

2 cups (480 ml) beef stock

1 (25-oz [740-ml]) bottle of full-bodied red wine, cabernet or merlot

2 medium shallots, finely chopped

2 cloves garlic, minced

2 tbsp (6 g) fresh parsley, chopped

Southeast Asian–Style Spicy Short Ribs

Many varieties of spicy, saucy beef like rendang are found in and around Malaysia and Singapore. This version reimagines a classic rendang as fall-off-the-bone short ribs with some outside influences.

Serves: 8
Sous vide cook time: 48 hours

Preheat the water bath to 144°F (62°C). In a large mixing bowl, add the brown sugar, soy sauce, orange juice, vinegar and hoisin sauce and whisk until the sugar dissolves, then add the lemongrass, ginger, red chilis, shallot and two-thirds of the scallions. Stir until it is combined, then split the mixture in half and pour into two separate vacuum bags.

Season the ribs with salt and pepper and add half of them to each bag and vacuum seal. Place the ribs in the sous vide bath and cook for 48 hours. Remove the bags, cut them open and pour the liquid contents through a sieve into a saucepan. Add the water to the pan and bring the liquid to a rolling boil, then reduce the heat to medium and simmer until the liquid reduces by half, about 15 minutes, then remove from the heat and set aside.

Turn the broiler to high and place the ribs, fat side up, in a pan. Broil the ribs until browned, about 2 to 3 minutes. Serve 1 rib per plate with jasmine rice, spooning the liquid reduction over the ribs and garnishing with sesame seeds and remaining scallions.

½ cup (110 g) brown sugar

1 cup (240 ml) low sodium soy sauce

¼ cup (60 ml) orange juice

¼ cup (60 ml) rice wine vinegar

¼ cup (60 ml) hoisin sauce

2 stalks lemongrass, crushed

1-inch (2.5-cm) piece ginger, peeled and minced

15–20 dried red chilis, split in half and seeded (leave the seeds if you want it extra spicy)

1 medium shallot, minced

3 scallions, thinly sliced, divided

4 lbs (1.8 kg) beef short ribs, cut into 8-oz (230-g) portions

Kosher salt

Black pepper

½ cup (120 ml) water

Jasmine rice, for serving

Toasted sesame seeds, for garnish

Beef Ramen

There is almost nothing more comforting than a bowl of colorful ramen. Thin-sliced beef tenderloin retains its suppleness and absorbs all the umami flavors of this deeply satisfying noodle soup.

Serves: 4

Sous vide cook time: 4 hours

Preheat the water bath to 134°F (56.6°C). Season the steaks with salt and pepper, and coat them with the togarashi rub. Vacuum seal and place into the sous vide bath for 4 hours.

In a large saucepan, heat 1 tablespoon (15 ml) of the grapeseed oil over medium-high heat and sauté the scallion whites until they soften, 5 to 6 minutes. Then add the garlic, sambal oelek and ginger and cook until fragrant, about 45 seconds. Add the broth, water, fish sauce and soy sauce. Bring to a boil and simmer for 15 to 20 minutes. Taste and adjust the seasoning as needed.

Remove the beef from the bag and dry with paper towels. Heat the remaining 2 tablespoons (30 ml) of grapeseed oil in a skillet over high heat and sear each fillet until browned on all sides, 2 to 3 minutes per side. Set the beef aside and allow to rest for 5 minutes, then thinly slice.

Add the noodles to the soup and cook per the directions on the packaging. Ladle the noodles and soup into four bowls. Garnish each bowl with 1 sliced steak, ¼ cup (25 g) of sprouts, half a soft-boiled egg, about ⅓ cup (45 g) mushrooms, a bok choy half and an even amount of carrots. Garnish with the scallion greens and serve.

4 beef tenderloin steaks, about 6 oz (170 g) each

Kosher salt

Black pepper

¼ cup (7 g) togarashi Japanese rub

3 tbsp (45 ml) grapeseed oil, divided

4 scallions, thinly sliced, white and green parts separated

2 cloves garlic, minced

1 tbsp (18 g) sambal oelek (Asian chili sauce)

1 tbsp (6 g) fresh ginger, minced

4 cups (1 L) beef broth

2 cups (480 ml) water

1 tbsp (15 ml) fish sauce

2 tbsp (30 ml) soy sauce

1 lb (455 g) ramen noodles

1 cup (100 g) bean sprouts, for serving

2 soft-boiled eggs, for serving

1½ cups (215 g) shiitake mushrooms, sliced and lightly sautéed, for serving

2 baby bok choy, halved and steamed, for serving

1 medium carrot, peeled and shredded, for serving

Veal Oscar

Named for Sweden's King Oscar II, who reportedly loved the combination of ingredients, this dish features thick-cut veal chops topped with crab, asparagus and a velvety béarnaise sauce.

Serves: 4

Sous vide cook time: 4 hours

Preheat the water bath to 134°F (56.6°C). Season the veal chops with salt and pepper. Place 2 veal chops, 1 clove of crushed garlic and 1 tablespoon (15 ml) of olive oil into each of the two bags. Place the bags into the water bath and cook for 4 hours.

During the last 15 minutes of cooking, melt the butter over medium-high heat in a sauté pan. Add the minced garlic and cook until fragrant, about 30 to 45 seconds. Add the crabmeat to the pan and cook, stirring frequently, for 5 minutes. Remove the pan from the heat and stir in the fresh parsley, cover and set aside.

Remove the veal chops from the bags and pat dry with paper towels. Heat the grapeseed oil in a cast-iron pan over high heat until smoking hot. Sear each veal chop until browned, about 2 minutes per side. Remove the chops to 4 separate plates, then top each with an even amount of crab meat. Serve with asparagus and drizzle with béarnaise sauce.

2 lbs (910 g) bone-in veal chops (4 chops)

Kosher salt

Black pepper

3 cloves garlic, 2 crushed, 1 minced, divided

2 tbsp (30 ml) olive oil

2 tbsp (28 g) butter, unsalted

8 oz (225 g) lump crab

2 tsp (2 g) fresh parsley, chopped

2 tbsp (30 ml) grapeseed oil

Butter and Garlic Asparagus (page 155), for serving

Béarnaise Sauce (page 176), for serving

Veal Roulades with Juniper Butter

This dish is served with a homemade compound butter inspired by the Nordic landscape. Juniper berries are used in northern European and Scandinavian cuisine to impart a sharp, clear flavor to dishes. These rolled veal steaks are stuffed with seasoned rye breadcrumbs, mushrooms and spinach.

Serves: 4

Sous vide cook time: 3 hours

One day before you plan on serving this meal, prepare the juniper butter and breadcrumbs. For the juniper butter, place the room-temperature butter into a bowl and, with a fork, mash the oregano, juniper, salt and pepper into the butter. Place the mixture onto parchment paper, roll it to form a log, cover and refrigerate.

Spread out the rye bread pieces on a rimmed baking sheet and let them sit at room temperature until dried out, 1 to 2 days. Place the bread in a large re-sealable plastic bag and seal, then lightly smash it with a kitchen mallet until it becomes fine, irregular crumbs. Heat the olive oil and butter in a skillet over medium heat until the butter begins to foam. Add the thyme and garlic and cook, stirring with a wooden spoon, until fragrant, about 1 minute. Add the crushed breadcrumbs and cook, stirring occasionally, until golden brown, about 4 minutes. Transfer to paper towels to allow it to drain, then season with salt. Let the breadcrumbs cool and put them in a closed container and set aside.

Preheat the water bath to 129°F (53.8°C). Lay plastic wrap on your work surface and place 1 of the veal cutlets on the plastic wrap, then put another layer of plastic over the cutlet. Using a kitchen mallet, gently pound the cutlet flat until it is 1/8 inch (3 mm) thick and set the meat aside. Repeat with the remaining cutlets.

In a skillet, heat the grapeseed oil over medium-high heat and add the mushrooms. Sauté the mushrooms, stirring frequently, until they begin to brown, about 8 to 10 minutes. Add the sliced shallots to the pan and cook until they become soft and translucent, 5 to 10 minutes. Then pour in the white wine, lower the heat to medium and cook until all the liquid has evaporated from the pan, about 10 minutes. Remove from the heat and allow it to cool.

Lay each cutlet out on plastic wrap and season with salt and pepper. Spread a layer of breadcrumbs onto each cutlet, then spread a layer of spinach and then the cooled mushrooms. Carefully roll each cutlet until you have a log shape, with the seam side down. Tie each roll securely with a few threads of kitchen twine. Place the rolls in a bag, vacuum seal and place into the sous vide bath. Cook for 3 hours.

Remove the cutlets from the bag and pat dry with paper towels. Heat the skillet over medium-high heat and add 2 tablespoons (17 g) of the juniper butter to the pan. When the butter is melted and foamy, sear the cutlets 3 minutes per side. Serve each roulade topped with a thin slice from the log of juniper butter.

Juniper Butter

¾ cup (180 g) unsalted butter, room temperature

½ tsp fresh oregano leaves, minced

1 tbsp (9 g) juniper berries, finely minced

¼ tsp kosher salt

¼ tsp white pepper

Breadcrumb Stuffing

2 cups (120 g) rye bread, cut into ½-inch (13-mm) cubes

¼ cup (60 ml) olive oil

4 tbsp (56 g) unsalted butter

2 tsp (2 g) thyme leaves, minced

2 cloves garlic, minced

Kosher salt

Veal

1 lb (455 g) veal cutlets (4 steaks)

2 tbsp (30 ml) grapeseed oil

2½ cups (170 g) cremini mushrooms, thinly sliced

2 small shallots, thinly sliced

¼ cup (60 ml) white wine

Kosher salt

Black pepper

1 cup (30 g) baby spinach, stems removed

Veal Pastrami

With some time and patience, you can prepare this indoor pastrami without the help of an outdoor smoker. This recipe utilizes a tough, inexpensive cut of veal and the sous vide turns it into a tender masterpiece.

Serves: 6 to 8

Sous vide cook time: 48 hours

In a stock pot bring the kosher salt, sugar, mustard seeds, coriander seeds, garlic, juniper berries, shallot, bay leaves, thyme and water to a boil. Remove from the heat and stir until all the salt and sugar has been dissolved, and set aside to cool. When the water cools to room temperature, stir in 1 ounce (30 ml) of the liquid smoke and the curing salt until it dissolves and place it into the refrigerator until it chills. Place your veal breast into the pot and be sure it is completely covered with the brine mixture. Cover and refrigerate the veal for at least 5 days.

Preheat the water bath to 150°F (65.5°C). In a bowl whisk the molasses, soy sauce and remaining 1 ounce (30 ml) of liquid smoke until fully mixed.

Remove the veal breast from the cure and rinse it off completely in cold water, removing any excess salt (discard the brine). Dry the veal breast with paper towels. Brush the molasses/soy sauce mixture over the entire veal breast, place it in a bag and vacuum seal it. Place it into the sous vide bath for 48 hours.

In a spice blender process the peppercorns, coriander seeds, brown sugar, juniper berries, pepper flakes, garlic powder and onion powder on high until the mixture is fully incorporated. Place the rub into an airtight container and store until the veal is finished.

Preheat the oven to 250°F (120°C). Remove the veal from the vacuum bag and discard the remaining contents. Transfer the veal onto a rack in a roasting pan and cover both sides of the breast completely with the spice rub. This step will give the roast the seasoning crust or "bark" that forms when using an outdoor smoker (see Note). Place the veal into the oven for 2½ to 3½ hours, until a crust forms, then remove from the oven. As an optional step, cover the pan completely with aluminum foil, poke a small hole into it, place the hose of a handheld smoker in and smoke it every 5 minutes for 30 minutes. Slice and serve with grain mustard or on a Rueben sandwich.

Note: If you own an outdoor smoker, you won't need the liquid smoke and you can skip the oven step. Place the veal into the smoker at 140°F (60°C) for 7 hours before serving.

Pastrami

1 cup (134 g) kosher salt

1 cup (200 g) granulated sugar

1 tbsp (9 g) mustard seeds

1 tbsp (5 g) coriander seeds

4 cloves garlic, crushed

1 tbsp (9 g) juniper berries

1 shallot, cut in half

2 bay leaves

4 sprigs thyme

2 quarts (1.9 L) water

2 oz (60 ml) liquid smoke, divided (see Note)

2 tbsp (30 g) pink curing salt

1 (5-lb [2.3-kg]) veal breast

4 oz (120 ml) molasses

2 oz (60 ml) low sodium soy sauce

Spice Rub

¾ cup (72 g) black peppercorns

¼ cup (20 g) coriander seeds

¾ cup (165 g) brown sugar

2 tbsp (19 g) juniper berries

¼ cup (6 g) red chili pepper flakes

2 tsp (7 g) garlic powder

2 tsp (5 g) onion powder

Grain mustard, for serving

Chapter 2

foolproof poultry & fowl

While proteins like chicken and duck can be deliciously moist and tender when prepared traditionally, the meat can also be easily overcooked and dry. The solution is the precise temperature control your sous vide provides. Don't believe me? Try the chicken breast, a notoriously tough cut if not handled gingerly. That's why sous vide is my favorite way to prepare my Blackened Chicken Maque Choux (page 45), Cambodian-Style Chicken Salad (page 58) and Spinach and Sundried Tomato– Stuffed Chicken Rolls (page 53) recipes.

Blackened Chicken Maque Choux

Spicy Cajun and comforting Creole flavors meet head-on in this delicious Southern chicken with corn and bell pepper medley stewed in heavy cream for an authentic bayou experience.

Serves: 4

Sous vide cook time: 2 hours

Preheat the water bath to 146°F (63.3°C). Thoroughly mix the paprika, salt, garlic powder, onion powder, cayenne pepper, black pepper, thyme and oregano in a bowl with a whisk. Season the chicken breast well on both sides with the mixture and place in a bag. Add the olive oil and vacuum seal. Place in the water bath and cook for 2 hours.

To make the maque choux, melt the butter in a heavy-bottomed skillet over medium-high heat, then add the onion and sauté until it is soft. Add the bell pepper, corn and fresh thyme, then cook an additional 6 to 7 minutes. Add the cream and hot sauce, lower the heat and simmer until it reduces and thickens a bit, 15 to 20 minutes. Remove from the heat, then add the scallions, parsley and basil; mix well and cover.

Remove the chicken from the bags when ready and dry it with paper towels. Heat the grapeseed or canola oil in a skillet over high heat and sear the chicken until brown, about 3 minutes per side. Allow the chicken to cool and cut into ½-inch (13-mm) cubes, then toss with the maque choux and serve.

1 tbsp (7 g) paprika

2 tsp (10 g) salt

1 tsp garlic powder

1 tsp onion powder

½ tsp ground cayenne pepper

2 tsp (4 g) black pepper

½ tsp dried thyme

½ tsp dried oregano

1½ lbs (680 g) whole boneless chicken breast

1 tbsp (15 ml) olive oil

2 tbsp (28 g) unsalted butter

1 small onion, finely chopped

1 small red bell pepper, finely chopped

5–6 ears of fresh corn, cut from the cob

2 tsp (2 g) fresh thyme leaves

1½ cups (360 ml) heavy cream

1 tbsp (15 ml) hot sauce

2 scallions, thinly sliced, green part only

2 tbsp (6 g) parsley, finely chopped

3 tbsp (8 g) basil, finely chopped

2 tbsp (30 ml) grapeseed or canola oil

Italian-Style Grilled Chicken Sandwich

I don't know about you, but I really love a hearty sandwich. And I adore the mix of flavors that can be found in Italian food culture. This tasty lunch makes the most of chicken breasts and dresses them up in roasted red peppers, arugula and balsamic vinegar.

Serves: 4

Sous vide cook time: 2 hours

Preheat the water bath to 146°F (63.3°C). Season the chicken cutlets with salt and pepper, place in a bag, vacuum seal and place the bag into the sous vide bath for 2 hours.

Before removing the chicken from the sous vide, bring a gas or charcoal grill to high heat.

Remove the chicken from the bag, pat dry with paper towels and brush the cutlets with 2 tablespoons (30 ml) of the olive oil. Grill the chicken until it is lightly charred, about 1 to 2 minutes per side. Slice each cutlet and place the meat from each cutlet on a toasted ciabatta roll. Top each chicken cutlet with sliced mozzarella, plum tomatoes, roasted pepper, arugula and spinach and drizzle with balsamic vinegar and 2 tablespoons (30 ml) of the olive oil. Cut the sandwiches in half and serve.

4 chicken cutlets, about 6 oz (170 g) each

Kosher salt

Black pepper

¼ cup (60 ml) olive oil, divided

4 (6-inch [15-cm]) toasted ciabatta rolls, for serving

8 oz (225 g) fresh mozzarella, thinly sliced, for serving

2 plum tomatoes, thinly sliced, for serving

1 medium roasted red bell pepper, thinly sliced, for serving

1 cup (20 g) arugula leaves, for serving

1 cup (30 g) baby spinach leaves, for serving

2 tbsp (30 ml) balsamic vinegar, for serving

Garlicky Chicken Thighs

Panamanian cuisine is diverse and consists of Spanish, American, Afro-Caribbean and indigenous influences. What makes me love this recipe is the unique combination of orange juice, allspice and sherry vinegar. This Central American roadside meal is heavy on garlic and wanderlust.

Serves: 8 to 10
Sous vide cook time: 2½ hours

Put the garlic cloves, salt and water into a food processor and blend into a paste. Add the bay leaves, orange juice, Worcestershire, vinegar, pepper and allspice, blending until smooth. Place the chicken thighs in a large bowl and pour in the marinade, mixing it to coat all the pieces. Cover and refrigerate for 12 hours.

Preheat the water bath to 165°F (73.8°C). Remove the chicken from the bowl, discard the marinade and divide the thighs into two bags. Vacuum seal the bags, without crowding the chicken. Submerge the sealed bags in the sous vide bath and cook for 2 hours and 30 minutes. When the chicken is done, grease grill grates with oil and heat until the oil begins to smoke. Remove the chicken from the bags and grill the chicken until it has a nice char on it, about 3 minutes per side, turning with a pair of tongs. Serve immediately with rice and sliced avocado.

20–25 cloves garlic

3 tbsp (25 g) kosher salt

3 tbsp (45 ml) water

2 bay leaves

1 cup (240 ml) orange juice

2 tbsp (30 ml) Worcestershire sauce

½ cup (120 ml) sherry vinegar

2 tbsp (17 g) black pepper

3 tsp (6 g) allspice, ground

10 boneless chicken thighs, about 6 oz (170 g) each

Rice and sliced avocado, for serving

Madras Curry Chicken

This deep red, spicy and redolent curry fusion dish is named for the city the British once called Madras but Indians now know as Chennai.

Serves: 4

Sous vide cook time: 2½ hours

Place the coriander, cumin, fenugreek, mustard and fennel seeds in a dry skillet over low heat. Roast the seeds gently, shaking the pan occasionally, until they begin to pop. When about half the seeds have popped, add the peppercorns, cardamom, cloves, cinnamon, turmeric, nutmeg, ginger and cayenne.

Continue to heat and stir gently until the mixture gets hot, but not burn. Pour into a dry herb blender, food processor or mortar and pestle. Grind into a powder. Let the mixture cool, then transfer to an airtight container and keep in a dry place for later use, up to 6 months.

In a bowl, mix the yogurt, lemon juice, 1 tablespoon (6 g) of ginger, ½ tablespoon (3 g) of Madras curry and salt. Cut the chicken into 1-inch (2.5-cm) cubes and put in a ziplock bag or covered bowl with the marinade, making sure all pieces are coated, then refrigerate for at least 12 hours.

Set your water bath to 149°F (65°C). While the water heats up, melt the ghee in a large saucepan over medium-high heat and add the shallots, 2 tablespoons (12 g) of ginger and chili pepper. Sauté until the shallots are soft, 8 to 10 minutes. Then add the garlic and cook for 1 minute. Stir in 1½ tablespoons (11 g) of the Madras curry and turmeric to coat the mixture, and then add the tomato sauce and cream. Stir until all ingredients are mixed, then simmer until the sauce thickens, 5 to 10 minutes.

Remove the pan from the heat, allow to cool for 10 minutes, then add salt and taste for any seasoning adjustment that you may want to make. Remove the chicken from the bowl, wipe off all excess marinade and put the chicken into a vacuum bag. Add the curry sauce to the bag and seal. Use a clip to secure the bag to the vessel you are using, to keep the bag from moving too much while the water is circulating. Cook for 2½ hours.

Once the chicken is cooked, place the raw spinach in a saucepan over low heat and pour the warm chicken and sauce over the spinach. Stir until the spinach wilts. Remove from the heat and serve hot over basmati rice.

Madras Curry Powder

8 tbsp (40 g) coriander seeds

8 tbsp (48 g) cumin seeds

2 tbsp (22 g) fenugreek seeds

1 tbsp (9 g) mustard seeds

1 tbsp (6 g) fennel seeds

8 tbsp (50 g) peppercorns

2 tbsp (6 g) whole green cardamom pods

1 tbsp (6 g) whole cloves

2 tbsp (15 g) ground cinnamon

2 tbsp (15 g) ground turmeric

1 tbsp (8 g) ground nutmeg

1 tbsp (5 g) ground ginger

1 tbsp (6 g) cayenne pepper

Chicken

1 cup (240 ml) Greek yogurt, strained

Juice of 1 lemon

3 tbsp (18 g) fresh ginger, minced, divided

Kosher salt

1½ lbs (680 g) boneless, skinless chicken breast

2 tbsp (28 g) ghee

2 medium shallots, minced

1–2 green or red chili peppers, seeds removed and thinly sliced

2 cloves garlic, minced

2 tsp (6 g) turmeric

1 cup (240 ml) tomato sauce

1½ cups (360 ml) heavy cream

3 cups (90 g) baby spinach

Basmati rice, for serving

Spinach and Sundried Tomato–Stuffed Chicken Rolls

Chicken breast is notorious for becoming dry when cooked by most methods. The sous vide takes the guesswork out of cooking moist, flavorful chicken breasts every time you prepare them by keeping the meat at a precise temperature in the water bath. Here I stuff some chicken roulades with comforting Italian flavors.

Serves: 4

Sous vide cook time: 2 hours

Butterfly the chicken breasts with a sharp knife angled parallel to the cutting board, slicing into one side of the chicken breast until you are about ½ inch (13 mm) from the other side. Fan out the chicken breasts on top of a piece of plastic wrap and cover it with another piece of plastic wrap. Use a kitchen mallet to flatten and tenderize the chicken breast evenly, taking extra care to not strike it hard enough to make any holes.

Next, place a chicken breast, uncut side down, on a fresh sheet of plastic wrap. Season with salt and pepper, then spread 1 ounce (28 g) each of the provolone and mozzarella cheese and 1 tablespoon (3 g) of tomatoes and top with one-quarter (11 g) of the spinach. Working from the narrower end (if there is one), roll up the chicken breast like you would a burrito, tucking in the sides and using the plastic wrap to tighten the roll as you go. Set aside on a plate and repeat the process with the other breasts. Refrigerate the roulades for 1 hour to allow them to set.

While the chicken is chilling, preheat the water bath to 149°F (65°C). Carefully unroll the chicken from the plastic wrap and put two chicken rolls in each of two bags. Place the chicken rolls far enough apart from each other that they will not touch when you vacuum seal the bag. Place the vacuum-sealed bags into the sous vide bath for 2 hours. Take the bags from the water, remove the roulades and dry them with paper towels. Heat your favorite marinara sauce in a saucepan 20 to 30 minutes before serving.

Heat the oil in a separate skillet over medium-high heat and quickly brown the chicken, 1 to 2 minutes per side. Spoon some marinara on each plate, place a roulade on the sauce and top with more marinara. Garnish with chopped basil and serve.

4 boneless, skinless chicken breasts, about 6 oz (170 g) each

1 tbsp (8 g) kosher salt

2 tsp (4 g) fresh black pepper

4 oz (115 g) sharp provolone, grated

4 oz (115 g) mozzarella, grated

¼ cup (14 g) sundried tomatoes, finely chopped

1½ cups (45 g) baby spinach, roughly chopped

Marinara sauce, for serving, optional

2 tbsp (30 ml) grapeseed oil

2 tbsp (5 g) fresh basil, chopped, for garnish

Chicken Shawarma with Pistachio Yogurt

This popular street food served in Israel and elsewhere in the Middle East is perfect for a lunch on the go. Whether thinly sliced or cubed, this tender coriander-spiced chicken on a warm flatbread with a cooling yogurt should always be on the menu.

Serves: 4 to 6

Sous vide cook time: 2 hours

In a large bowl, combine the lemon juice, smoked paprika, turmeric, cumin, coriander, cinnamon, pepper flakes, salt, black pepper, minced garlic and olive oil, whisking together until fully incorporated. Pour the marinade into a large ziplock bag, then add the sliced onion and chicken to the bag. Mix well, until all the pieces are coated evenly, then refrigerate for 12 hours.

Preheat the oven to 350°F (177°C). Spread the pistachios on a nonstick sheet pan and roast for 8 to 10 minutes until golden brown (see Note). Cool the pistachios, then put the pistachios, lemon zest and garlic in a food processor and process on low until everything is fully ground. Stream in the olive oil and process until the mixture is smooth and no longer grainy, then season with a little salt and pepper. In a separate bowl, combine the yogurt, lemon juice, salt and pepper, then fold the pistachio mixture into the yogurt and mix well. You can thin the yogurt mixture with a bit more olive oil if needed. Taste for seasoning, cover and refrigerate while the chicken is prepared.

Preheat the water bath to 146°F (63.3°C). Remove the chicken and onions from the marinade bag and place both into a sous vide bag, vacuum seal it and submerge in the water bath for 2 hours. Heat a frying pan over high heat and add the grapeseed oil. When the pan is smoking hot, sear the chicken on each side until it is browned, about 1 minute per side. Remove the chicken to a cutting board and slice it thinly crosswise. Reduce the heat to medium-high and sauté the onions until browned, about 10 to 15 minutes.

Set up the pita bread on plates and, in each, place equal portions of the chicken, sautéed onions, cucumber, tomato, lettuce, parsley and a healthy dollop of pistachio yogurt sauce.

> **Note:** To produce a smoother pistachio paste, peel and discard the outer skin of the pistachios before toasting.

Juice of 2 lemons

2 tsp (5 g) smoked paprika

1 tbsp (7 g) turmeric

1 tbsp (7 g) cumin powder

2 tsp (4 g) ground coriander

½ tsp cinnamon

2 tsp (3 g) red pepper flakes

2 tsp (10 g) salt

2 tsp (5 g) ground black pepper

4 cloves garlic, minced

½ cup (120 ml) olive oil

1 large onion, thinly sliced

2 lbs (910 g) boneless, skinless chicken breast

2 tbsp (30 ml) grapeseed oil

4–6 small pita breads

1 cucumber, finely diced

2 plum tomatoes, finely diced

½ cup (20 g) shredded lettuce

½ cup (30 g) fresh parsley, chopped

Yogurt Sauce

1 cup (150 g) raw pistachios

1 tsp lemon zest

1 clove garlic, minced

¼ cup (60 ml) olive oil

1½ cups (370 g) Greek or whole-milk yogurt

Juice of 1 lemon

½ tsp kosher salt

½ tsp black pepper

Djaj Bil-Bahar Il-Asfar (Persian Spiced Chicken)

Heavy on garlic and spices such as chilis, cumin seeds and, most notably, the mouthwatering tang of sumac, this Middle Eastern chicken dish is dry-rubbed and cooked until tender before finishing over a charcoal grill.

Serves: 8

Sous vide cook time: 2 hours

In a dry sauté pan over medium heat, add the whole cloves, allspice, peppercorns, dry chili peppers, cumin seeds and coriander seeds. Continuously shake the pan until you begin to hear the seeds pop, about 2 minutes. Remove from the heat and pour the contents into a spice grinder with the rose hips, if using. Add the salt, sumac, cinnamon, ginger, nutmeg, fenugreek, garlic, cardamom and curry powder. Grind until all toasted seeds are converted into powder and all spices are fully incorporated. Place the spice mix in a large bowl and whisk in the olive oil until it becomes a smooth paste. Toss the chicken thighs in the mixture until fully coated, then cover and refrigerate for 8 hours.

Preheat the water bath to 165°F (73.8°C). Vacuum seal the marinated chicken in a bag and place it in the water bath for 2 hours. Once done, remove the chicken from the bag and pat dry, without rubbing away the surface spices.

Grease the grates of a grill with oil and heat to high heat. Place the chicken on the grill and cook until the meat is browned and the skin has a light char on it, about 3 to 4 minutes per side. Remove the chicken from the heat and serve with rice or flatbread.

4 whole cloves

4 allspice berries

2 tsp (5 g) black peppercorns

4 dried chiles de arbol

2 tsp (4 g) cumin seeds

2 tsp (4 g) coriander seeds

4 dried rose hips, optional

2 tsp (6 g) kosher salt

1 tbsp (8 g) sumac

1 tbsp (8 g) cinnamon

1 tbsp (6 g) fresh ginger, minced

1½ tsp (3 g) fresh grated nutmeg

2 tsp (7 g) ground fenugreek

10 cloves garlic, mashed into a paste

6 cardamom pods

1 tbsp (7 g) mild curry powder

½ cup (120 ml) olive oil

3½ lbs (1.6 kg) boneless chicken thighs (about 8 pieces)

Rice or flatbread, for serving

Cambodian-Style Chicken Salad

This delicious salad brings all the hallmarks of Cambodian and Vietnamese cooking onto one bright, savory plate with hints of fresh mint, citrusy lime and a light touch of spiciness from fresh chilis.

Serves: 4

Sous vide cook time: 2 hours

Preheat the water bath to 149°F (65°C). Season the chicken with salt and pepper, vacuum seal in a bag and cook for 2 hours.

In a small bowl whisk the water, lime juice, sugar, fish sauce, garlic and grapeseed oil until the sugar is dissolved and fully incorporated. Refrigerate.

When the chicken is done, remove it from the bag and cut into ½-inch (13-mm) cubes or use two forks to shred it.

In a large mixing bowl, toss the mint, cabbage, carrots, onion, chili pepper and chicken with the dressing until fully coated. Top with sesame seeds, peanuts and crispy shallots and garnish with whole mint leaves to serve.

1 lb (455 g) chicken breast

½ tsp kosher salt

¼ tsp black pepper

4 tbsp (60 ml) water

2 tbsp (30 ml) fresh lime juice

2 tbsp (24 g) granulated sugar

2 tbsp (30 ml) fish sauce

1 clove garlic, minced

2 tbsp (30 ml) grapeseed oil

⅓ cup (30 g) fresh mint, chiffonade

4 cups (280 g) red cabbage, shredded

3 medium carrots, thinly julienned

½ cup (58 g) red onion, thinly sliced

1 red chili pepper, minced

2 tbsp (20 g) sesame seeds, toasted

¼ cup (40 g) peanuts, crushed

3 tbsp (30 g) crispy shallots

Whole mint leaves, for garnish

Pan-Seared Duck Breast with Pomegranate Dressing

Take some of the uncertainty out of cooking perfect duck breasts with this method. Then dress your field salad up in pomegranate seeds and let the duck be the star of this simple plate. The tartness of the pomegranate dressing complements the rich flavor of the duck and crispy texture of the skin.

Serves: 2

Sous vide cook time: 2 to 4 hours

Preheat the water bath to 134°F (56.6°C). While the water is heating, score the duck breasts on the skin/fat side using a small sharp knife. Slice the skin and fat off the breasts in a crosshatch or diamond pattern at a 45-degree angle without cutting into the meat, about ½ inch (13 mm) apart. Season the duck with salt and pepper.

Put the garlic flakes and 2 sprigs of thyme in a bag, add the seasoned duck breasts, then vacuum seal. Place in the water bath for a minimum of 2 hours (4 hours maximum).

While the duck is cooking, toss together the salad greens and red onion, then cover and refrigerate. Place the pomegranate juice, lemon juice, orange juice, honey, shallot, garlic and remaining sprig of thyme into a blender and process until the mixture is well combined. Slowly drizzle the olive oil into the mixture as it blends. Taste before adding salt and pepper, then blend for another 15 to 20 seconds. Transfer to a closed container and refrigerate for at least 1 hour to allow flavors to incorporate.

To complete the dish, carefully remove the vacuum bag from the hot water, take the duck breasts out of the bag and pat them dry with paper towels. Heat up a cast-iron skillet over high heat and add the grapeseed oil. When the oil gets hot and begins to shimmer, add the duck, skin side down. Only sear the skin side to crisp the skin; the fatty barrier will insulate against the meat cooking any further (do not sear the meat side or you risk overcooking the duck). Sear for 4 to 5 minutes, then remove from the heat and allow the duck to rest 5 minutes before slicing.

Add the salad to the plates, drizzle with dressing and garnish with pomegranate seeds and green onions. Top with the sliced duck breast and serve.

2 duck breasts, about 6 oz (170 g) each

Kosher salt

Ground pepper

1 tbsp (10 g) dried garlic flakes

3 sprigs fresh thyme, divided

6 cups (200 g) salad greens

2 tbsp (20 g) red onion, thinly sliced

¼ cup (60 ml) pomegranate juice

Juice of ½ lemon

Juice of 1 navel orange

2 tsp (10 ml) honey

1 small shallot, finely minced

1 clove garlic, roughly chopped

¾ cup (180 ml) olive oil

1 tbsp (15 ml) grapeseed oil

3 tbsp (32 g) pomegranate seeds, for garnish

2 tbsp (12 g) green onion, thinly sliced, for garnish

Note: This meal can be served with any greens of your choice. Good examples are arugula, mâche, radicchio, escarole and watercress or a combination of any of those greens.

Duck Leg Confit

Hailing from the Basque region of France, Confit de Canard (duck cooked in fat) is arguably one of those classic French dishes that is popular across the entire country. Originally a method for preserving poultry, now it's used to make a deliciously tender dish.

Serves: 4

Sous vide cook time: 36 hours

Preheat the water bath to 155°F (68.3°C). Trim off any excess fat from the duck legs and season with the salt and pepper. Put the duck legs in a bag, add the rendered fat and vacuum seal the bag or use the water displacement method. Place the bag in the water and cook for 36 hours, adding more hot water over time as it evaporates.

Carefully take the bag out of the water bath and very gently remove the duck legs from the bag because the meat will be fall-off-the-bone tender. You can also allow the bag to cool and refrigerate the duck for later use. The duck legs can be reheated in the oven at 425°F (220°C) or placed under a broiler. To crisp the skin, broil for 5 to 6 minutes or use a kitchen torch with a Searzall attachment. Serve with Honey-Glazed Heirloom Carrots.

4 duck legs, about 8 oz (225 g) each

Kosher salt

Black pepper

1 cup (240 ml) rendered duck or goose fat

Honey-Glazed Heirloom Carrots (page 151), for serving

Sriracha-Glazed Duck with Pineapple Salsa

This glazed duck breast balances sweet and citrusy flavors of molasses and orange juice with the fiery chili spiciness of Sriracha sauce.

Serves: 4

Sous vide cook time: 4 hours

Heat the sous vide bath to 134°F (56.6°C). In a mixing bowl combine the pineapple, bell pepper, red onion, cilantro, jalapeño pepper, garlic, a pinch of salt and the lime juice. Toss until completely mixed, then cover and refrigerate.

Using a sharp knife, carefully score the duck skin in a crosshatch pattern without cutting into the meat. Season with salt and pepper, then place the duck breasts in a single layer into a vacuum bag with the thyme and garlic. Vacuum seal and place into the sous vide bath for 4 hours.

During the last 30 minutes of cooking, make the glaze. In a small saucepan over medium-high heat, stir the molasses, honey, Sriracha, orange juice, red pepper flakes and soy sauce. Bring the mixture to a boil, then lower to a simmer and cook until the mixture becomes thickened and syrupy, 10 to 12 minutes. Remove from the heat, cover and set aside.

Remove the duck from the vacuum bag and pat dry with paper towels. Heat the grapeseed oil in a skillet over medium-high heat, then add the duck breast, skin side down, and sear until some of the fat renders and the skin is browned, about 3 to 4 minutes.

Transfer the duck to a pan, skin side up, and brush the glaze onto the breast, then place the duck under a broiler until the glaze caramelizes, about 1 to 2 minutes. Allow the duck to rest on a cutting board for 5 minutes before slicing. Serve each duck breast topped with the pineapple salsa.

2 cups (330 g) fresh pineapple, chopped

1 cup (150 g) red bell pepper, finely chopped

¼ cup (40 g) red onion, finely chopped

½ cup (8 g) cilantro, finely chopped

1 medium jalapeño, seeded and minced

1 clove garlic, minced

Kosher salt

¼ cup (60 ml) fresh lime juice

4 duck breasts, about 6 oz (170 g) each

Black pepper

2 sprigs thyme

1 clove garlic, crushed

¼ cup (60 ml) molasses

¼ cup (60 ml) honey

3 tbsp (45 ml) Sriracha chili sauce

¼ cup (60 ml) fresh orange juice

1 tsp red pepper flakes

2 tbsp (30 ml) soy sauce

2 tbsp (30 ml) grapeseed oil

Chapter 3

perfectly poached pork

Cooking pork can be tricky using traditional methods. The risk of overcooking it is high, while undercooking pork will not be very appetizing to your dinner guests. No worries, though, as the immersion circulator will give you that perfectly juicy (and safe) pork chop—and ribs and sausage and tenderloin—every time.

Feijoada (Portuguese Stew)

Stew up some beef, pork belly, Portuguese pork sausages and black beans in this stick-to-your-ribs, slow-cooked Brazilian national dish. Feel free to use the types of meats you like for this stew—it's all a matter of personal preference. Here I combine a trifecta of sausages from three different regions of South America.

Serves: 8 to 10
Sous vide cook time: 48 hours

Rinse and soak the black beans in cool, clear water for at least 6 hours before cooking.

Preheat the water bath to 176°F (80°C). Heat the grapeseed oil over medium-high heat in a heavy-bottomed frying pan. Season the short ribs and pork belly with salt and pepper. Add the short ribs to the pan and brown, 3 minutes per side, adding more oil as needed, then remove from the pan, cover and set aside. Next, place the pork belly into the pan you just used for the short ribs and cook on all sides until it becomes somewhat crisp, 3 minutes per side. Remove from the heat, pat dry with a paper towel and allow to cool, then slice crosswise into 1-inch (2.5-cm) pieces. Pour all but 2 tablespoons (30 ml) of the oil out of the pan. Return the pan to the heat and add the onions. Cook, stirring frequently, until they are soft and translucent, about 5 minutes, then add the garlic and cook until fragrant, about 1 minute. Remove the pan from the heat and allow the mixture to cool.

Drain the beans. In each of two bags, place ¼ pound (115 g) of each type of sausage, ¼ pound (115 g) of smoked pork shank, 2 cups (385 g) of black beans, 3 cups (720 ml) of water, half of the onion mixture, 1 pound (455 g) of beef ribs and ½ pound (225 g) of sliced pork belly. Use your hands to mix the contents of each bag, then vacuum seal and place into the sous vide bath for 48 hours. I recommend using a chamber sealer for this step (see Note).

Thirty minutes before the stew is finished, make the farofa. Melt the butter in the frying pan, and add the onion and poblano pepper and sauté until soft and slightly browned, 8 to 10 minutes. Add the garlic and stir frequently until aromatic, about 1 minute. Add the cassava flour and stir with a wooden spoon until the entire mixture is golden brown and toasted, 6 to 8 minutes. Remove from the heat and allow it to cool.

When the stew is finished, carefully remove the bags from the water and place them into a large bowl. Take extra care when moving the bags to the bowl, as the long cook time and high temperature could have weakened the structural integrity of the bags. Cut the bags open and dump the contents into a large pot. If the liquid is too thin for your taste, remove 1½ cups (680 g) of the beans to a bowl and mash them, then stir them back into the stew. Serve the feijoada over rice alongside orange slices and topped with parsley and the farofa.

> **Note:** DO NOT use freezer bags for this recipe because they can fail at the seams and allow water into the bag. I recommend that you use a chamber sealer and double the vacuum bags due to the high temperature and long cook time.

1½ lbs (680 g) dry black beans, rinsed and soaked

3–4 tbsp (45–60 ml) grapeseed oil

2 lbs (910 g) beef short ribs, cut into 3-inch (7.5-cm) pieces

1 lb (455 g) pork belly, 1 inch (2.5 cm) thick

Kosher salt

Black pepper

2 large onions, chopped

8 cloves garlic, thinly sliced

½ lb (225 g) or 2 large links Argentinian chorizo sausage, cut into 1-inch (2.5-cm) slices

½ lb (225 g) or 2 large links Colombian chorizo sausage, cut into 1-inch (2.5-cm) slices

½ lb (225 g) or 2 large links linguiça (Brazilian sausage), cut into 1-inch (2.5-cm) slices

½ lb (225 g) smoked pork shank, thinly sliced

6 cups (1.5 L) water

Farofa (optional)

6 tbsp (85 g) unsalted butter

1 large onion, chopped

1 large poblano pepper

2 tbsp (18 g) garlic, minced

2 cups (255 g) cassava flour

Rice, for serving

Orange slices, for serving

½ cup (30 g) fresh parsley, finely chopped, for serving

Pernil

This juicy pork shoulder is popular throughout Latin America and the Caribbean. It is usually shredded and served alongside black beans and rice, but can also be enjoyed with yucca, Pickled Red Onions (page 179) or fried plantains at family gatherings in Cuba, Puerto Rico and the Dominican Republic. Leftovers can be used in Cubano sandwiches (page 73) for a quick lunch option during the week.

Serves: 10 to 12

Sous vide cook time: 36 hours

With a sharp knife, score the pork in a crosshatch pattern all over, paying extra attention to the skin (the same way you would do a holiday ham or whole duck), and tie it with kitchen twine every 2 inches (5 cm).

In a food processor, process the sofrito, garlic, sazón, adobo, oregano and black pepper on high until the mixture is smooth.

Place the roast into a large ziplock bag, pour the marinade into it and move it around with your hands until the roast is entirely coated in the marinade. Refrigerate for 12 to 24 hours.

Preheat the water bath to 165°F (73.8°C). Put the marinated pork roast into a vacuum bag and seal it, then place it into the sous vide bath for 36 hours.

Toward the end of the sous vide cook time, preheat the oven to 425°F (220°C). Carefully remove the pork roast from the bag, pat it dry and place it in a roasting pan. Roast for 1 to 1½ hours until the skin becomes dark brown and crisp when you tap it with a spoon. Remove the roast from the oven and allow it to rest for 10 to 15 minutes. Peel the skin from the meat and set aside for serving. Using two large forks, shred the meat and place on a large platter with the crispy skin and serve with rice and beans or tostones.

8 lbs (3.6 kg) pork shoulder, bone-in and skin on

12 oz (340 g) sofrito

15 cloves garlic, roughly chopped

3 packets sazón seasoning

1 tbsp (10 g) adobo seasoning

1 tbsp (3 g) dried oregano

1 tbsp (8 g) black peppercorns, crushed with a mortar and pestle

Rice and beans or tostones, for serving

Note: At high temperatures, vacuum bags can become very soft and their structural integrity can become compromised. You will want to consider how to remove the bag from scalding water safely. Try using tongs to retrieve the bag and having a pot ready for immediate transfer.

Miami Cubano Sandwich

The "Cubano" is an easy-to-prepare lunch or weeknight meal and it makes good use of your leftover pernil roast. This sandwich has a delicious combination of pernil, sliced deli ham and Swiss cheese on a baguette toasted in a sandwich press for a delightful finishing touch.

Serves: 4

Sous vide cook time: 36 hours

Split the baguettes, brush the cut sides with some melted butter and place in a skillet one at a time, cut side down, for 2 minutes, until lightly browned. Spread a thin layer of mustard on the toasted half of each sandwich, then top each with 2 slices of ham, 6 ounces (170 g) of pernil, sliced pickles and 2 slices of cheese. Close the sandwich and gently press it to flatten it slightly. Brush the top and bottom of the sandwich with melted butter and place it into a sandwich press with moderate pressure and cook until toasted, about 8 to 10 minutes. Remove sandwiches from the press, allow them to cool slightly and serve.

> **Note:** If you do not have a sandwich press, you can use two heavy-bottomed skillets. Add the sandwich to one heated pan and use the bottom of the other to flatten it. When toasted on one side, flip and warm the other side until toasted.

4 (6-inch [15-cm]) pieces of baguette

¼ cup (56 g) butter, melted

¼ cup (60 g) mustard

8 slices (220 g) deli ham

1½ lbs (680 g) Pernil (page 70)

2–3 Dill Pickles, thinly sliced lengthwise (page 180)

8 slices (220 g) Swiss cheese

Iberico Pork Tenderloin with Cherry–Mustard Sauce

If you are not usually a pork eater, Iberico pork will likely convert you with its unique nutty-flavored meat. If you are already a fan, you will love this tenderloin highlighting meat from the more mountainous regions of Spain.

Serves: 4
Sous vide cook time: 3 hours

Preheat the water bath to 140°F (60°C). Tie the tenderloin with kitchen twine until it forms a neat cylinder; this will help it maintain shape throughout the cooking process. Season the pork with salt and pepper. Place the pork into a vacuum bag with the crushed garlic, thyme and olive oil, then seal. Place the bag into the sous vide bath for 3 hours.

During the last hour of cooking, prepare the sauce. In a mixing bowl whisk the dry mustard and water until the mixture is smooth, then set aside. In a saucepan over medium-high heat, bring the cherries, sugar, vinegar, port and 1 teaspoon salt to a boil, stirring occasionally, until the mixture becomes a bit syrupy, about 10 to 15 minutes. Remove the pan from the heat and puree the mixture with an immersion blender until smooth. Return the pan to the heat and boil the mixture until it thickens, about 5 to 7 minutes. Remove from the heat and carefully whisk the mixture into the bowl with the mustard until fully incorporated. Cover and set the sauce aside while you finish the pork.

Remove the tenderloin from the bag and pat dry with paper towels. Heat the grapeseed oil over high heat and quickly sear the tenderloin on all sides until browned, 3 minutes per side. Use a knife to remove the kitchen twine. Slice the tenderloin and plate, drizzled with the cherry–mustard sauce to serve.

1 (2-lb [910-g]) Iberico pork tenderloin (domestic pork can be used as a substitute)

Kosher salt

Black pepper

2 cloves garlic, crushed

2 sprigs thyme

1 tbsp (15 ml) olive oil

2 tbsp (22 g) Coleman's dry mustard

1 tbsp (15 ml) water

3 cups (460 g) stemmed and pitted cherries

3 tbsp (36 g) granulated sugar

½ cup (120 ml) red wine vinegar

¼ cup (60 ml) port wine

2 tbsp (30 ml) grapeseed oil

Sausage and Peppers

One of the fondest food memories I have from my youth is the mouthwatering aromas of deep fried zeppoles and sausages during the Feast of San Gennaro celebration in my neighborhood. The immersion circulator helps to retain the valuable juices in this recipe for sweet and spicy Italian sausages.

Serves: 4

Sous vide cook time: 3 hours

Preheat the water bath to 150°F (65.5°C). Place the chicken stock and sausages in a vacuum bag and seal. Place the bag in the water bath and cook for 3 hours.

During the last hour of cooking, heat 3 tablespoons (45 ml) of the olive oil in a sauté pan over medium-high heat. Add the onions, peppers, oregano, salt and pepper and toss until all are coated with oil. Sauté the vegetables until they soften, about 15 minutes. Transfer the vegetables to a plate, cover and keep warm.

Remove the sausages from the bag and dry with paper towels. Heat the remaining 2 tablespoons (30 ml) of oil in the skillet over high heat and quickly brown the sausages on all sides, 3 to 4 minutes per side. Place the sausages on a cutting board and allow them to cool. Slice the sausages on the bias into 2-inch (5-cm) pieces, and place the sliced sausage back into the skillet and toss with the onions and peppers. Add an equal amount of sausage and pepper mixture to each roll and serve.

¼ cup (60 ml) chicken stock

1½ lbs (680 g) Italian pork sausage, 3 sweet and 3 spicy links

5 tbsp (75 ml) olive oil, divided

2 large onions, julienned

2 medium red bell peppers, julienned

2 medium green bell peppers, julienned

2 tsp (2 g) dried oregano

Kosher salt

Black pepper

4 Italian rolls, toasted

Sweet and Spicy Soy-Glazed Pork Chops

Honey and Sriracha chili sauce add sweetness, spiciness and big flavor, while the sous vide method helps maintain the succulence of these double-cut pork chops.

Serves: 4

Sous vide cook time: 4 hours

Preheat the water bath to 145°F (62.7°C). Season the pork chops with salt and pepper, vacuum seal them in bags (maximum 2 per bag) and place them in the water bath to cook for 4 hours.

In a medium-size bowl, whisk the tahini, vinegar, soy sauce, honey and Sriracha until completely blended; set aside. Heat 2 tablespoons (30 ml) of olive oil in a small saucepan over medium heat. Add the garlic, stirring often, until it begins to brown, 1 to 2 minutes. Then whisk in the liquid ingredient mixture. Continue to whisk over medium heat until the sauce thickens into a glaze, 5 to 10 minutes. Remove the glaze from the heat, cover it and set it aside while you finish the pork.

When the pork chops are finished cooking, remove them from the bags and pat dry with paper towels. Heat the remaining 2 tablespoons (30 ml) of oil in a cast-iron pan over high heat until the oil is smoking hot, then sear the pork chops until browned on all sides. Allow them to rest for 5 minutes and serve drizzled liberally with the glaze.

4 double-cut, bone-in pork chops, about 1 lb (455 g) each

½ tsp kosher salt

½ tsp black pepper

2 tbsp (32 g) tahini

2 tbsp (30 ml) white wine vinegar

¼ cup (60 ml) soy sauce

4 tbsp (60 ml) honey

2 tbsp (30 ml) Sriracha chili sauce

4 tbsp (60 ml) olive oil, divided

3 cloves garlic, finely chopped

Lemongrass Pork Ribs

In this recipe, a marinade of lemongrass and fish sauce, two staples of Southeast Asian cooking, tenderizes the ribs and infuses the meat with flavor. This delectable dinner takes its inspiration from Cambodia and Vietnam.

Serves: 4 to 6

Sous vide cook time: 24 hours

With a sharp knife split the rack of ribs in half and scrape the silver skin from the back of the ribs with a spoon.

In a medium bowl whisk the oil, sugar, soy sauce, fish sauce and liquid smoke until the sugar dissolves. Put the liquid mixture in a food processor, then add the lemongrass, chili paste, shallots, five-spice powder, garlic, ginger and salt and process until smooth. Place the ribs into a ziplock bag or vacuum bag and pour the seasoning mixture into the bag, then move the ribs around in the bag to coat them. Vacuum seal the bag and refrigerate overnight.

Preheat the water bath to 145°F (62.7°C). Place the bag with the ribs into the water and cook for 24 hours.

Prepare the lemongrass sauce 1 hour before removing the ribs from the sous vide. In a medium saucepan bring the fish sauce, lime juice, sugar, lemongrass and water to a boil and stir until the sugar dissolves and the mixture reduces a bit. Remove the sauce from the heat and allow it to cool, then stir in the carrot, chilies and cilantro and set aside.

Preheat a grill or broiler to a high setting. Remove the ribs from the bag and pat them dry with paper towels. Grill the ribs until they are browned, with a slight char, 3 to 5 minutes. If using a broiler, keep the ribs at least 6 inches (15 cm) away from the flame and broil until browned. Remove the ribs from the heat and garnish with chives. Serve with a side of lemongrass sauce for dipping.

Ribs

4 lbs (1.8 kg) baby back pork ribs

2 tbsp (30 ml) canola oil

2 tbsp (28 g) brown sugar

2 tbsp (30 ml) soy sauce

1 tbsp (15 ml) fish sauce

½ tsp liquid smoke, optional

2 tbsp (28 g) lemongrass paste

1 tbsp (18 g) sambal oelek (hot chili paste)

2 medium shallots, minced

2 tsp (5 g) Chinese five-spice powder

4 cloves garlic, chopped

2 tbsp (12 g) ginger, minced

2 tsp (6 g) kosher salt

Chopped chives, for garnish

Lemongrass Sauce

¼ cup (60 ml) fish sauce

2 tbsp (30 ml) fresh lime juice

¼ cup (50 g) granulated sugar

2 tbsp (28 g) lemongrass paste

1 cup (240 ml) water

½ carrot, shredded

3 red Thai chili peppers, thinly sliced

2 tbsp (2 g) cilantro, chopped

"Roasted" Pork Belly

Minimal dry seasonings and a long cook time is the key to preparing the most succulent pork belly slab that, once removed from the water bath, is ready to crisp under a broiler or kitchen torch.

Serves: 4 to 6

Sous vide cook time: 24 hours

Preheat the water bath to 154°F (68°C). Using a sharp paring knife, poke holes into the skin of the pork belly without going deep enough to puncture the meat. Season the pork with salt and pepper, then place in a bag and vacuum seal. Place the bag into the water bath and cook for 24 hours.

Prepare the sauce 1 hour before the pork belly is done. In a small saucepan over medium-high heat, bring the hoisin sauce, soy sauce, rice wine, honey, sugar, sesame oil, garlic, Sichuan pepper and Chinese five-spice powder to a boil. Lower the heat and simmer, stirring occasionally, until it thickens, 10 to 15 minutes. Remove the sauce from the heat, cover and keep warm.

When the pork belly is finished, remove it to a pan and dry with paper towels. Brown the pork belly with a kitchen torch and Searzall attachment until the skin becomes brown and crisp. Alternatively, set a broiler to high and place the pork, skin side up, under the heat until the skin browns and crisps, 4 to 5 minutes. Remove the pork to a cutting board and brush it with the glaze. Slice thinly and serve garnished with scallions.

2 lbs (910 g) pork belly, split in half

Kosher salt

Black pepper

¼ cup (60 ml) hoisin sauce

¼ cup (60 ml) soy sauce

2 tbsp (30 ml) Shaoxing wine (Chinese rice wine)

1 tbsp (15 ml) honey

1 tbsp (14 g) brown sugar

2 tsp (10 ml) sesame oil

1 clove garlic, minced

1 tbsp (8 g) Sichuan peppercorns, crushed with a mortar and pestle, optional

½ tsp Chinese five-spice powder

2 scallions, thinly sliced, for garnish

Pork Cutlets with Marsala Wine and Wild Mushrooms

These poached pork chops go well with the bit of sweetness from the wine, while the earthy flavor of wild mushrooms balances it all out.

Serves: 4

Sous vide cook time: 3 hours

Preheat the water bath to 140°F (60°C). Brush the pork cutlets with 1 teaspoon of the balsamic vinegar, then season with salt and pepper. Put the cutlets, in a single layer, in a vacuum bag and seal it. Place it into the sous vide bath and cook for 3 hours.

Preheat the oven to 375°F (190°C). Place the garlic on a nonstick baking pan and coat each clove with the olive oil. Bake until the cloves are golden brown, 30 to 45 minutes. Remove the garlic from the oven and set it aside.

In a medium-sized bowl place the dried porcini and chanterelle mushrooms and cover with lukewarm water. Allow the mushrooms to steep 40 to 50 minutes. Strain the mushroom liquid through a sieve into a bowl, making sure to get any grit out of the liquid. Rinse the mushrooms, saving the strained liquid; set both aside.

In a large skillet over medium-high heat, melt 2 tablespoons (28 g) of the butter. Remove the pork from the bag and dry with paper towels. Sear the chops until browned, about 2 minutes per side. Place the cutlets aside and cover to keep warm.

In a small bowl whisk the cornstarch and cold water together until fully combined. Melt the remaining tablespoon (14 g) of butter in the same pan and add the reconstituted mushrooms. Cook the mushrooms, stirring frequently, for 5 minutes, then deglaze the pan with the wine, scraping up any browned bits from the bottom of the pan. Add the thyme, rosemary, veal or chicken stock, ¼ cup (60 ml) of the mushroom liquid, the roasted garlic cloves, ground juniper berries, cornstarch mixture and remaining teaspoon of vinegar to the pan. Bring the liquid to a boil and reduce it by half, about 5 to 10 minutes or until it thickens. Add salt and pepper to taste, then remove the pan from the heat. Place a pork cutlet on each plate and serve with mushrooms and sauce spooned on top.

4 boneless pork cutlets, about 6 oz (170 g) each

2 tsp (10 ml) balsamic vinegar, divided

Kosher salt

Black pepper

8–10 cloves garlic

1 tbsp (15 ml) olive oil

1 oz (28 g) dried porcini mushrooms

1 oz (28 g) dried chanterelle mushrooms

1½ cups (360 ml) lukewarm water

3 tbsp (42 g) butter, divided

2 tsp (5 g) cornstarch

2 tsp (10 ml) cold water

⅓ cup (60 ml) marsala wine

1 sprig fresh thyme

1 sprig fresh rosemary

⅓ cup (60 ml) veal or chicken stock

6–8 juniper berries, crushed in a mortar and pestle

Chapter 4

luscious lamb

Pasture-raised lamb is one of my favorite proteins. I would describe the flavor as somewhat gamey, but fresh tasting. The meat becomes even more tender and flavorful when prepared via the sous vide method. Once you serve your dinner guests the recipes in this section, they will scramble for future invitations.

Cumin-Spiced Lamb Burger

It's the sous vide pickled red onions included in this dish that really liven up the burger by cutting through the essential fattiness of lamb and complementing the cumin and garlic flavors.

Serves: 4

Sous vide cook time: 2½ to 4 hours

Prepare the aioli by mashing the garlic and the salt in a mortar and pestle until a paste forms. Place in a small bowl and whisk in the mayonnaise, olive oil and lemon juice. Season to taste with salt and pepper, then refrigerate until ready to use.

Preheat the water bath to 130°F (54.4°C). In a large bowl, gently mix the lamb, cumin, salt and pepper, then form the mixture into four evenly sized patties and place in a bag. Vacuum seal the patties, without letting them touch each other inside the bag, and place into the water bath for 2½ to 4 hours.

Remove the patties from the bag and dry with paper towels. Heat the oil in a pan over high heat until it is smoking hot and quickly brown each patty, 2 minutes per side. Place each burger onto a toasted bun and top with a spoonful of aioli and a heap of pickled onions to serve.

Garlic Aioli

2 cloves garlic, pressed into a paste

½ tsp kosher salt

½ cup (120 g) mayonnaise

2 tbsp (30 ml) olive oil

1 tbsp (15 ml) fresh lemon juice

Black pepper

Lamb Burger

1½ lbs (680 g) ground lamb

1 tbsp (7 g) ground cumin

2 tsp (6 g) kosher salt

2 tsp (5 g) black pepper

2 tbsp (30 ml) grapeseed oil

4 hamburger buns, toasted

4 oz (115 g) Pickled Red Onions (page 179)

Lamb Necks with Saffron Couscous

Relatively tough cuts of lamb or mutton are made buttery and delicious through the sous vide method and served with a delicately seasoned grain kicked up a notch with a pinch of saffron.

Serves: 2 to 4

Sous vide cook time: 24 hours

Preheat the water bath to 134°F (56.6°C). In a small bowl whisk the paprika, cumin, black pepper, coriander, cinnamon, nutmeg, cardamom, cloves and salt until fully incorporated. Season the lamb with the spice mixture, put it in a ziplock bag or in a bowl with a cover and refrigerate for 4 to 6 hours. Then, place the lamb in a bag, add the olive oil, vacuum seal and lower into the water bath. Cook for 24 hours.

Thirty minutes before the lamb is done, place the couscous in a saucepan and set aside. Heat the butter over medium heat in a skillet and add the shallots and raisins; sauté until the shallots are soft and translucent, 5 to 10 minutes. Add the stock and saffron to the skillet and bring to a rolling boil. Remove the skillet from the heat and pour the stock, raisins and shallots into the saucepan with the couscous. Mix well with a spoon and cover for 15 minutes at room temperature. Fluff with a fork, season with salt and pepper, then garnish with chopped mint (if using) before serving.

Heat the grapeseed oil in a skillet over medium-high heat. Remove the lamb from the vacuum bag and dry with paper towels. Sear until it is browned on all sides, 3 minutes per side. Serve with saffron couscous.

2 tsp (5 g) smoked paprika

2 tsp (4 g) ground cumin

1 tsp freshly ground black pepper

1 tsp ground coriander

½ tsp ground cinnamon

½ tsp ground nutmeg

¼ tsp ground cardamom

¼ tsp ground cloves

1 tsp kosher salt

2 lbs (910 g) lamb necks

2 tbsp (30 ml) olive oil

1 cup (175 g) dried couscous

2 tbsp (28 g) butter, unsalted

¼ cup (40 g) shallots, finely chopped

½ cup (80 g) golden raisins

1¼ cups (300 ml) chicken stock

¼ tsp saffron threads

2 tsp (4 g) chopped fresh mint, for garnish, optional

2 tbsp (30 ml) grapeseed oil

Grilled Leg of Lamb with Gjetost Sauce

While it can be daunting to tackle a whole leg of lamb, the sous vide takes much of the guesswork out of this feat. Be ready for a multi-day marinade and cook, and then be prepared for the accolades. A sweet–savory Norwegian cheese (pronounced yay-toast) finishes this Nordic delicacy.

Serves: 8 to 10

Sous vide cook time: 24 to 36 hours

In a large container or stockpot, mix the buttermilk, rosemary, bay leaf, salt, garlic powder and pepper well. Score the lamb in a crosshatch pattern with a sharp knife, being careful not to slice too deep into the meat, only through the top surface of the fat. Lower the leg of lamb into the buttermilk mixture and roll it to coat well. Cover and refrigerate for at least 24 and up to 48 hours, flipping the lamb at least four times during this period to keep it coated.

Preheat the water bath to 134°F (56.6°C). Remove the lamb from the marinade, rinse it with cold water and pat dry with paper towels, removing any excess marinade. Put the lamb in a bag, then vacuum seal the bag and place in the water bath for 24 to 36 hours.

Start the sauce about an hour before you want to serve dinner. Melt the butter in a saucepan over medium-high heat, then add the flour and whisk continuously until it forms a medium-brown roux that resembles the color of peanut butter. Remove from the heat and blend in the light cream with a whisk or stick blender until smooth. Add the chicken stock, bring to boil, then lower the heat to medium and continue whisking and cooking until it has thickened a bit, about 5 minutes. Mix in the Gjetost cheese.

In a bowl, whisk some of the sauce into the sour cream to temper, then return the entire mixture back to the saucepan and stir to blend. Add the salt and white pepper to taste and stir in the minced fresh dill. Cover and keep warm until ready to serve.

Fifteen minutes before removing the lamb from the sous vide, heat up a grill to high and grease the rack with grapeseed oil. When the oil is smoking, brown the lamb on all sides, 5 to 10 minutes per side, then remove from the heat and allow it to rest for 10 minutes before carving. Serve topped with Gjetost sauce and with the side of your choice.

Notes: To create a more even cook on your lamb, have your butcher remove the rump, French cut the bone and loosen the meat from the bone.

Norwegian Gjetost cheese can be found in specialty cheese shops, and at some grocery stores, including Fairway and Whole Foods.

Lamb

1 gallon (4 L) buttermilk

4 sprigs rosemary, finely chopped

1 large bay leaf

1 tbsp (20 g) salt

2 tsp (7 g) garlic powder

2 tsp (5 g) fresh ground pepper

1 (6-lb [2.7-kg]) bone-in leg of lamb

2 tbsp (30 ml) grapeseed oil

Gjetost Sauce

2 tbsp (28 g) unsalted butter

2 tbsp (15 g) flour

¾ cup (180 ml) light cream, room temperature

½ cup (120 ml) chicken stock

1 cup (120 g) Gjetost cheese, grated

½ cup (115 g) sour cream

Kosher salt

White pepper

2 tbsp (7 g) fresh dill, minced

Rack of Lamb with Butter and Garlic Asparagus

Australia and New Zealand raise some particularly beautiful sheep, so let's make an equally impressive rack of lamb in their honor. When cooked sous vide, the lamb maintains its juiciness and intense earthy flavors.

Serves: 4

Sous vide cook time: 4 hours

Preheat the water bath to 134°F (56.6°C). Season the lamb with salt and pepper. In each of two vacuum bags, add 2 sprigs of rosemary; half of the olive oil, garlic and onion flakes; and 1 rack of the lamb, then seal. Place the bags into the sous vide bath and cook for 4 hours.

Remove the lamb from the bags and discard the remaining contents (unless you are making a gravy), and pat the lamb dry with paper towels. Oil grill grates with the grapeseed oil and brown the lamb over high heat, about 2 to 3 minutes per side. Allow the lamb to rest 5 minutes before slicing and serving with the Butter and Garlic Asparagus.

2 lbs (910 g) rack of lamb (2 racks), trimmed of fat and silver-skin

Kosher salt

Black pepper

4 sprigs fresh rosemary

¼ cup (60 ml) olive oil

1 tbsp (10 g) dried garlic flakes

1 tbsp (7 g) dried onion flakes

2 tbsp (30 ml) grapeseed oil

Butter and Garlic Asparagus (page 155), for serving

Grilled Lamb Chops with Tomato-Prune Sauce

It's the vinegar-laced marinade that gives this lamb and onion dish a distinctive sour note. The tomato and prune sauce provides the perfect sweetness for a balanced plate.

Serves: 2

Sous vide cook time: 4 hours

In a medium bowl whisk the seltzer; vinegar; 2 teaspoons (4 g) each of coriander, paprika, cumin; ¼ teaspoon salt; the pepper and half of the dill until fully incorporated.

Place the lamb chops and onion wedges into a ziplock bag and pour in the marinade. Use your hands to make sure all of the contents are coated completely. Seal the bag and place into the refrigerator for 12 to 24 hours.

Preheat the water bath to 134°F (56.6°C). Remove the lamb from the marinade and save the onion wedges in a covered bowl for later use, then discard the remaining marinade.

Put the lamb in a vacuum bag in a single layer and seal. Place it into the sous vide bath for 4 hours.

During the final hour of cooking, prepare the sauce. Heat the grapeseed oil in a saucepan over medium-high heat, then add the chopped onion and cook, stirring frequently, until they are soft and translucent, 5 to 6 minutes. Add the garlic and cook for 30 to 45 seconds, until fragrant. Add the tomato paste, a heaping tablespoon (5 g) each of coriander and paprika, ½ teaspoon of cumin, the pepper flakes, prunes, a pinch of kosher salt and black pepper. Cook the mixture, stirring frequently, until it begins to caramelize, 4 to 5 minutes. Pour the can of crushed tomatoes into the pan, reduce the heat to medium and simmer until it thickens, about 20 minutes, then stir in the remaining dill and the parsley, cilantro and lemon juice. Remove it from the heat and cover.

Remove the lamb from the vacuum bags and pat dry with paper towels. Oil the grill grates and set to high. Grill the marinated onions wedges until they soften and are slightly charred, 8 to 10 minutes, then remove them to four plates. Grill the lamb chops 2 to 3 minutes per side until browned. Assemble the lamb chops on the plates with the onion wedges and spoon the sauce over each steak to serve.

½ cup (120 ml) seltzer water

2 tbsp (30 ml) white vinegar

1 tbsp plus 2 tsp (10 g) coriander powder, divided

1 tbsp plus 2 tsp (9 g) paprika, divided

2½ tsp (6 g) cumin, divided

½ tsp salt, divided

½ tsp black pepper

5 sprigs dill, minced, divided

4 lamb shoulder chops, about 8 oz (225 g) each

3 small onions, 2 cut into small wedges and 1 chopped, divided

2 tbsp (30 ml) grapeseed oil

6 cloves garlic, minced

¼ cup (65 g) tomato paste

1 tsp red pepper flakes

20 prunes, pitted and chopped

1 (28-oz [795-g]) can crushed tomatoes

¼ cup (15 g) parsley, finely chopped

½ cup (8 g) cilantro, finely chopped

1 tbsp (15 ml) lemon juice

Lamb Shanks with Garlic Mashed Potatoes

Rather than pay inflated restaurant prices, you can create impressive, flavorful lamb shanks at home. This fashionably Milanese recipe is fork tender and rich. The lamb, after many hours of slow cooking in the sous vide bath, becomes tender to the bone while developing a luxurious savory flavor, especially when aromatics like garlic and herbs are added to the bag prior to cooking.

Serves: 4

Sous vide cook time: 48 hours

Preheat the water bath to 143°F (61.6°F). Season the shanks with salt and pepper. In each of two bags, put 2 lamb shanks, 1 teaspoon (6 g) each of dried onion and garlic flakes, ½ teaspoon each of dried thyme and oregano and ¼ cup (60 ml) of olive oil. Place the bags into the water bath and cook for 48 hours.

Prepare the gravy 30 minutes before removing the lamb. In a saucepan over medium-high heat, melt 1 tablespoon (14 g) of butter, then add the onion. Cook the onion for 3 minutes until it softens. Add the remaining 3 tablespoons (42 g) of butter to the pan and whisk until melted. Pour in the flour and continue whisking until the mixture is light brown in color. Add the garlic and cook for 30 seconds until fragrant, then add the beef stock, vinegar and red wine. Bring the mixture to a boil, then lower the heat to a simmer. Cook the mixture, stirring frequently, until it thickens, 10 to 15 minutes. Remove the pan from the heat, cover and keep warm.

Remove the bags from the water bath and allow to cool for 10 minutes before opening them. Remove the lamb from the bags and discard the remaining contents (see Note). Carefully place the lamb shanks into a large roasting pan or sheet pan and pat dry with paper towels. Place the pan under a broiler for 4 to 5 minutes until browned. If using a kitchen torch, brown the meat with a high heat setting while constantly moving the flame to avoid burning the meat or creating an unpleasant flavor. Serve with mashed potatoes.

> **Note:** For more intensely flavored gravy, the liquid from the bags can be strained and stirred into the gravy.

4 lamb shanks, about 1 lb (455 g) each

Kosher salt

Black pepper

2 tsp (12 g) dried onion flakes

2 tsp (12 g) dried garlic flakes

1 tsp dried thyme

1 tsp dried oregano

½ cup (120 ml) olive oil

4 tbsp (56 g) butter, divided

1 large onion, chopped

3 tbsp (24 g) all-purpose flour

2 cloves garlic, minced

¾ cup (180 ml) beef stock

1 tbsp (15 ml) red wine vinegar

¾ cup (180 ml) full-bodied red wine

Garlic Mashed Potatoes (page 160), for serving

Chapter 5

superb seafood

Most seafood is so delicate that overcooking with traditional techniques can lead to a tough chew. But cooking your fish and mollusks sous vide ensures that your dishes remain moist, flavorful and vibrant. No longer will you need to worry about rubbery shrimp, lobster or scallops; you only get perfection!

Lobster Fettuccine in Herbed Cream Sauce

Even if you think you've had tender lobster before, just wait until you poach the crustacean in butter in this nod to the cuisine of Northern Italy. Perfetto!

Serves: 6 to 8

Sous vide cook time: 1 hour

Preheat the water bath to 131°F (55°C). Place the butter, chili paste, crushed garlic and parsley into a vacuum sealer bag. Season the lobster with salt, then add the lobster to the bag and vacuum seal. Lower the bag into the pot and allow it to cook for 1 hour while you make the sauce and pasta.

For the sauce, heat the oil in a heavy-bottomed large saucepan over high heat. Add the reserved lobster shells and sauté the shells for about 3 minutes. Reduce the heat to low, stir in the tomato paste and continue stirring for 5 more minutes. Add the tomatoes, wine, vinegar, sliced garlic, thyme, parsley, salt and pepper and simmer for 4 to 5 minutes until the alcohol from the wine cooks out. Add the cream and bring to a boil, then reduce the heat to medium-low. Stirring occasionally, simmer the sauce just until lobster flavor infuses the cream and the sauce slightly thickens, about 20 minutes.

Strain the sauce into a fresh saucepan with a cheesecloth or sieve, pressing on the solids to extract as much liquid as possible, then put the saucepan over low heat. Make any seasoning adjustments and simmer 5 to 10 minutes for the sauce to thicken. Remove the pan from the heat. Cook and drain the pasta per directions on the box.

Remove the lobster from the water bath and empty the vacuum sealer bag, saving only the lobster and 2 tablespoons (30 ml) of the liquid, discarding any herbs left in the bag. Cut the tails into small bite-size pieces and add to the sauce along with the cooking liquid, tossing to coat. Add the cooked pasta to the saucepan. Toss it all together until completely covered in sauce and serve garnished with basil leaves.

Note: Setting your water temperature to 131°F (55°C) and cooking for 1 hour yields a tender and succulent end result. For a more traditional texture, but a still perfectly cooked lobster, set the temperature to 140°F (60°C) and cook between 30 and 45 minutes.

8 tbsp (120 g) unsalted butter

1 tbsp (16 g) chili paste

3 cloves garlic, 1 crushed, 2 sliced, divided

2 sprigs parsley

1.8 lbs (815 g) frozen lobster tails, thawed and removed from shells (reserve the shells)

1 tsp salt

3 tbsp (45 ml) olive oil

¼ cup (65 g) tomato paste

2 plum tomatoes, chopped

½ cup (120 ml) dry white wine

2 tbsp (30 ml) white wine vinegar

1 sprig fresh thyme

1 tbsp (3 g) fresh parsley, chopped

Black pepper

4 cups (1 L) whipping cream

1 lb (455 g) fettuccine or pasta of your choice

4 large basil leaves, finely chopped, for garnish

Pacific Salmon with Citrus Kale Salad

Known throughout the world as one of the most desirable wild-caught fish, salmon is endemic to the Pacific Northwest. In this dish, it is given a light smoky flavor and served with tangy bitter greens. In this recipe, I like to use a handheld smoker before sealing the fish. This device adds a nice amount of smoky flavor to the salmon.

Serves: 2

Sous vide cook time: 45 minutes

Preheat the water bath to 125°F (51.6°C). Season the salmon with salt, pepper and garlic powder, then place in a deep bowl and cover with plastic wrap or foil. Poke a small hole in the plastic or foil, place a smoking gun hose into the hole and pump smoke into it 3 times, allowing 5 minutes in between pumps. Once sufficiently smoked, place the salmon into a vacuum bag with the scallions and seal. Cook the fish for 45 minutes in the sous vide while you prepare the salad.

In a bowl, combine the lemon juice and salt. Slowly whisk in the olive oil until incorporated. Add the crushed garlic cloves and set aside to allow the flavors to infuse the oil. Roll the kale leaves together in batches and slice them into strips (chiffonade). Toss the kale, cheese and walnuts together in a large bowl. Discard the garlic cloves from the dressing, add half of the dressing to the salad and toss again to coat everything well. Taste and adjust the seasoning if necessary. Divide the salad evenly onto 2 plates, top each with a salmon filet and serve immediately.

2 salmon filets, about 8 oz (225 g) each

½ tsp garlic powder

2 scallions, whole

⅓ cup (80 ml) freshly squeezed lemon juice

1 tsp kosher salt

1½ cups (360 ml) extra-virgin olive oil

5 cloves garlic, crushed

2 cups (130 g) kale leaves, trimmed of stems, washed and dried

1½ cups (150 g) freshly grated Parmesan

½ cup (60 g) toasted walnuts, chopped

Mediterranean Octopus Salad

Nothing says the Greek Islands like a delightful salad of chickpeas, feta and fresh-from-the-sea octopus. The grilled tender tentacles make a hearty and healthy dish.

Serves: 4

Sous vide cook time: 5 hours

Preheat the water bath to 171°F (77.2°C). Make an ice bath and bring a large pot of water to boil. Blanch the octopus in the boiling water, about 15 minutes. Remove it from the pot and immediately place it in the ice bath for 5 minutes. When the octopus cools, season it with salt and place it in a bag with the garlic flakes and ¼ cup (60 ml) of olive oil, then vacuum seal it. Place the bag in the water bath and cook for 5 hours. During the last hour of cooking, prepare the salad.

Add the chickpeas, cucumber, roasted bell pepper, tomatoes, parsley, feta cheese, red onion and basil to a large mixing bowl and toss to combine, then cover and refrigerate. In a small mixing bowl, whisk together the balsamic vinegar, lemon juice, garlic, Dijon, salt and pepper, and slowly drizzle ½ cup (120 ml) of olive oil into the bowl until it is fully incorporated. Cover and refrigerate.

Prepare another ice bath. Remove the bag from the water bath and place it into the ice bath for 15 to 20 minutes until the octopus is completely cool. Take the octopus from the bag, cut into 1-inch (2.5-cm) pieces and toss it with the salad vegetables. Drizzle the reserved dressing into the salad, toss again and serve.

1½ lbs (680 g) fresh octopus

2 tbsp (20 g) dried garlic flakes

¾ cup (180 ml) olive oil, divided

2 (15-oz [425-g]) cans chickpeas, drained

1 large cucumber, chopped

½ cup (75 g) roasted red bell pepper, chopped

2 plum tomatoes, seeded and chopped

¼ cup (15 g) fresh parsley

8 oz (225 g) feta cheese, crumbled

½ cup (58 g) diced red onion

¼ cup (10 g) basil, finely chopped

¼ cup (60 ml) white balsamic vinegar

2 tbsp (30 ml) lemon juice

2 cloves garlic, minced

1 tsp Dijon mustard

1 tsp kosher salt

1 tsp pepper

Monkfish with Saffron Buerre Blanc

Monkfish, once maligned as a trash fish and tossed back into the sea by fishermen, rose to relative popularity as "poor-man's lobster" due to its taste and texture being similar to the pricier crustacean. When paired with tangy and creamy beurre blanc, this lobster imposter gets away with it.

Serves: 4

Sous vide cook time: 30 minutes

Preheat the water bath to 132°F (55.5°C). Season the monkfish filets with salt and pepper, put them in two bags, vacuum seal and refrigerate for 30 minutes. Drop the bags in the water and cook for 30 minutes while you prepare the beurre blanc sauce.

Add the shallot, white wine and vinegar to a small saucepan over medium-high heat. Simmer until it reduces to about 2 tablespoons (30 ml) and has a syrupy consistency, 8 to 10 minutes. Add the cream and saffron and season with the salt and white pepper, then boil for 1 minute. Reduce the heat to low and begin to whisk in the cold butter one cube at a time, while occasionally lifting the pan from the heat to cool the mixture a bit (this prevents the sauce from breaking). When all the butter is incorporated, remove from the heat, strain the mixture through a sieve, then stir in the lemon juice and add more salt and pepper to taste.

Remove the fish from the bags and pat dry. If you would like to sear the fish, add the grapeseed oil to a skillet over medium-high heat and cook 1 minute per side to brown (see Note). Serve sliced and topped with the beurre blanc sauce.

> **Note:** The fish is ready to serve straight out of the bag. Searing it is optional and may result in overcooking if the heat is too high or the fish is left in the pan for longer than 1 minute per side.

Fish

4 skinless monkfish filets, about 8 oz (225 g) each

1 tsp kosher salt

1 tsp black pepper

2 tbsp (30 ml) grapeseed oil, optional

Beurre Blanc

1 small shallot, finely chopped

¼ cup (60 ml) dry white wine

¼ cup (60 ml) champagne vinegar

¼ cup (60 ml) heavy cream

½ tsp saffron threads

¼ tsp kosher salt

⅛ tsp white pepper

1 cup (230 g) cold unsalted butter, cut into cubes

2 tsp (10 ml) fresh lemon juice

Dill Salmon

The star of this Scandinavian dish is obviously the salmon, cooked to the ideal temperature to stay flaky and moist. Paired with amazing buttery root vegetables made popular in Norwegian kitchens, this dish is comfort food heaven.

Serves: 4

Sous vide cook time: 45 minutes

Preheat the water bath to 123°F (50.5°C). Season the fish with salt and pepper, then place in a vacuum bag in a single layer with the scallions, dill and olive oil and seal. Cook for 45 minutes. Remove the salmon from the bag and pat dry with paper towels. Heat the butter in a sauté pan over medium-high heat until it stops foaming, then sear the salmon fillets until browned, about 30 seconds per side. Serve with Buttery Root Vegetables.

4 salmon filets, skin on, about 6 oz (170 g) each

Kosher salt

Black pepper

2 scallions

4 dill sprigs, plus 2–3 more for garnish

2 tbsp (30 ml) olive oil

1 tbsp (14 g) unsalted butter

Buttery Root Vegetables (page 159), for serving

Drunken Rose Red Snapper

Firm white fish filets poached in a mixture of Asian rose wine and a rich fish stock gives this snapper some amazing floral notes along with a light savory flavor. This dish makes for a great spring or summer dinner.

Serves: 4

Sous vide cook time: 30 minutes

Preheat the water bath to 130°F (54.4°C) while beginning the fish stock. Clean and filet the fish, discarding the innards. Set aside the filets, then add the remainder of the fish to a large saucepan over high heat. Add the onion, 3 whole cloves garlic, carrots, celery, thyme, peppercorns, bay leaf, salt and water and bring the liquid to a boil. Lower the heat to medium and simmer until the mixture reduces to about 2 cups (480 ml), about 25 to 30 minutes. Strain the stock through a sieve into a container, discard the solids and set the stock aside.

In a sauté pan, heat the canola oil over medium-high heat and add the shallots. Cook the shallots, stirring occasionally, until they are soft and slightly browned, 8 to 10 minutes. Add the 2 cloves of minced garlic and cook until fragrant, about 45 seconds, then pour in the fish stock and wine (see Note). Bring the liquid to a boil, lower the heat to medium and simmer for 15 minutes (this cooks the alcohol from the wine out of the mixture). Remove the pan from the heat and allow the liquid to cool to room temperature.

Season the snapper filets lightly with salt and pepper. Place the filets into a vacuum bag in a single layer; pour in the wine mixture and seal. Place into the sous vide bath and cook for 30 minutes. Remove the bag, cut it open and drain the liquid back into the saucepan. Using a fish spatula, gently remove the fish from the bag with the skin side down, then plate and spoon the broth onto the fish. Top with scallions to serve.

2 (2-lb [910-g]) whole red snappers

1 large onion, quartered

5 cloves garlic, 3 whole and 2 minced, divided

2 medium carrots, peeled and roughly chopped

2 celery hearts, roughly chopped

3 sprigs fresh thyme

10 black peppercorns

1 bay leaf

1 tsp kosher salt

6 cups (1.5 L) water

2 tbsp (30 ml) canola oil

2 medium shallots, chopped

1 cup (240 ml) Chinese rose wine (Mei Kuei Lu Chiew)

2 scallions, thinly sliced, for serving

Note: The wine can be added ahead of the stock (carefully) and flambéed to remove the alcohol. However, I only recommend this for experienced cooks. Mei Kuei Lu Chiew (Chinese wine) has a very high alcohol content; use with caution.

Scallops à l'Américaine

Gently poached scallops are the perfect complement to wine and cognac in this French seafood dish.

Serves: 4 to 6

Sous vide cook time: 30 minutes

Preheat the water bath to 123°F (50.5°C). Season the scallops with salt and pepper, place into a vacuum bag in a single layer, add 4 tablespoons (56 g) of the butter and seal. Place the bag into the sous vide bath for 30 minutes.

While the scallops cook, prepare the sauce. Melt 2 tablespoons (28 g) of the butter in a saucepan over medium-high heat and add the sliced shallots. Sauté the shallots until they are soft and translucent, 30 seconds. Then add the garlic and cook until fragrant, 30 to 40 seconds. Add the wine and cognac, then simmer until the liquid reduces a bit, 2 to 3 minutes. Stir in the tomatoes and tomato paste until fully incorporated. Season with salt and cayenne pepper and simmer for 10 more minutes. Remove the pan from the heat and stir in the crème fraîche, cover and set aside.

Take the bag from the sous vide bath, remove the scallops and discard the remaining contents. Melt the remaining 2 tablespoons (28 g) of butter in a sauté pan over medium-high heat until it stops foaming. Sear each scallop for 20 to 30 seconds per side. Spoon the sauce onto plates and place the desired number of scallops on each plate. Garnish with chopped chives and serve with crusty French bread.

1 lb (455 g) large sea scallops (about 15–20 pieces)

Kosher salt

Black pepper

8 tbsp (112 g) unsalted butter, divided

2 large shallots, thinly sliced

2 cloves garlic, minced

½ cup (120 ml) dry white wine

3 tbsp (45 ml) cognac

1 (14.7-oz [417-g]) can diced tomatoes

2 tsp (10 g) tomato paste

¼ tsp cayenne pepper

¼ cup (60 ml) crème fraîche

Chopped chives, for garnish

French bread, for serving

Goan Shrimp

This recipe hails from India's smallest, yet richest state, Goa, which is in western India, where fish curries are wildly popular. Tender shrimp is nestled in a mild and creamy tomato curry with some unexpected accompaniments like hard-cooked eggs and coconut.

Serves: 4

Sous vide cook time: 1 hour

Preheat the water bath to 134°F (56.6°C). In a food processor blend the coconut, dried chilis, tamarind, ginger, garlic, onion, turmeric, cumin, coriander, salt, pepper and water on high until it becomes smooth, adding more water as needed. Set aside.

Season the shrimp with salt and pepper and place them into a vacuum bag in a single layer and seal. Place the shrimp into the sous vide bath and cook for 1 hour.

While the fish is cooking, prepare the sauce. In a large saucepan add the oil over medium-high heat. When the oil is hot, add the shallots and minced chilis and sauté until the shallots are soft and translucent, then add the tomatoes. Cook the mixture for 5 minutes, then stir in half of the reserved curry paste (see Note) and lower the heat to medium. Allow the sauce to simmer 6 to 7 minutes, then pour in the coconut milk and stir until it is fully incorporated. Taste the sauce for seasonings and add salt or pepper as needed (more paste can also be added if desired). Simmer for 15 minutes and remove from the heat.

Remove the shrimp from the bag and stir them into the slightly cooled sauce. Serve with basmati rice and hard-boiled eggs and garnish with cilantro.

> **Note:** The unused curry sauce can be used in another recipe, or vacuum sealed and frozen for up to 3 months.

Goan Curry Paste

2 cups (160 g) fresh shredded coconut

5 dried Goan chilis or red chili peppers, stemmed and seeded

1 tbsp (15 g) tamarind paste

1 (1-inch [2.5-cm]) piece fresh ginger, minced

5 cloves garlic, minced

1 small onion, finely chopped

½ tsp ground turmeric

½ tsp cumin

1 tsp ground coriander

1 tsp kosher salt

½ tsp black pepper

1 cup (240 ml) water

Shrimp Curry

1 lb (455 g) large shrimp, shells removed

Kosher salt

Black pepper

2 tbsp (30 ml) grapeseed oil

2 shallots, chopped

3 green chilis, minced

2 medium tomatoes, seeded and chopped

1 (13.5-oz [400-ml]) can coconut milk

Basmati rice, for serving

4 hard-boiled eggs, for serving

¼ cup (4 g) cilantro, chopped, for garnish

Sea Bass in Tuscan Kale

If there was ever a way to make Chilean sea bass even more buttery and moist, this is it. Wrapping the delicate fish, along with mushrooms and leeks, in a hearty Lacinato kale, creates a beautiful serving-size package for each of your guests.

Serves: 4

Sous vide cook time: 35 minutes

Preheat the water bath to 131°F (55.2°C), and bring a separate large pot of water to a boil and make an ice bath. One at a time, blanch the kale leaves for 3 minutes and submerge them immediately into an ice bath. After 5 minutes in the ice bath, remove the kale carefully so you don't rip the leaves and pat dry with paper towels. Set them aside and allow them to warm to room temperature.

Season the sea bass with ½ teaspoon of the salt and pepper, then bag and vacuum seal the fish, immerse it in the sous vide bath and cook for 35 minutes.

While the fish cooks, heat 2 tablespoons (30 ml) of the oil over medium-high heat in a large sauté pan, then add the mushrooms and sprinkle with ½ teaspoon of salt. Cook until the mushrooms release their water and the pan begins to dry out, about 10 minutes. Add the remaining tablespoon (15 ml) of oil to the pan followed by the tomato and leek and cook until they soften, about 10 to 15 minutes. Lower the heat to medium, then add the garlic, spinach and arugula in batches until they are completely wilted. Remove the vegetables from the heat and cover the pan to keep warm. Lay the kale leaves out on your work surface with the top side of the leaves face down (the "top," or inside, of the leaf is darker green and has less prominent ribs). Add a spoonful of vegetable mixture to the center of each leaf.

Take the vacuum bag out of the water bath, remove the filets and place each one in the center of its own kale leaf on top of the sautéed vegetables. Spread an even amount of the remaining vegetable mixture onto and around the filets. Fold the leaves over the fish, end over end, forming a small package, and serve seam side down.

4 large Lacinato kale leaves, bottom stems and large ribs removed

4 skinless sea bass filets, about 6 oz (170 g) each

1 tsp kosher salt, divided

½ tsp black pepper

3 tbsp (45 ml) grapeseed or olive oil, divided

7 oz (200 g) shiitake mushrooms, thinly sliced

1 plum tomato, seeded and finely diced

1 large leek, rinsed and thinly sliced (white and pale green parts only)

2 cloves garlic, minced

8 oz (225 g) baby spinach

8 oz (225 g) arugula

Chapter 6

sensational small plates & starters

Your sous vide device can help turn your appetizers and small plates into amazing tasting works of art. Surprised? This versatile kitchen tool can handle a large variety of small meals. This section spotlights the globally delicious versatility of cooking small plates with an immersion circulator.

Moroccan-Style Sticky Meatballs

The blend of honey, cinnamon, lemons, cloves and coriander enrobe juicy lamb meatballs in a delicious North African glaze.

Serves: 4

Sous vide cook time: 2 hours

Preheat the water bath to 140°F (60°C). Prepare the glaze by bringing the honey, cilantro, lemon juice, vinegar, ketchup, soy sauce, 1 clove crushed garlic, anise, cinnamon, peppercorns, ginger, cardamom, whole cloves, chili flakes and ½ teaspoon salt to a simmer over medium-high heat. Allow the mixture to simmer, whisking occasionally, until the sauce is reduced to about 1 cup (240 ml) and has thickened, about 15 minutes. Pour through a sieve into a bowl. Cover and set aside.

Soak the bread in the milk, then remove and squeeze out any excess liquid. Mix together the bread, ground meat and egg until incorporated. Add 1 teaspoon of salt, pepper, 4 cloves minced garlic, nutmeg, ginger, turmeric, paprika, cayenne, ground cloves, coriander and cumin. Mix well with your hands to distribute the seasoning. Add 3 tablespoons (11 g) each of parsley, cilantro and scallion, and knead for a minute. With your hands, roll the mixture into small round balls about 1½ inches (4 cm) in size and place on a parchment-lined sheet pan. Place the meatballs in the freezer for 1½ to 2 hours so they can firm up.

Remove the meatballs from the freezer and vacuum seal them in a bag in a single layer. Place the meatballs in the sous vide bath and cook for 2 hours. Heat the grapeseed oil over medium-high heat and fry the meatballs until browned, about 2 minutes per side. Using a kitchen brush, coat the meatballs on all sides with the glaze, then sprinkle the remaining parsley on top before serving.

1 cup (240 ml) honey

½ cup (8 g) fresh cilantro sprigs

⅓ cup (80 ml) lemon juice

¼ cup (60 ml) rice vinegar

¼ cup (60 ml) ketchup

¼ cup (60 ml) soy sauce

5 cloves garlic, divided

1 whole star anise

1 cinnamon stick

1 tsp black peppercorns

1 tbsp (6 g) ginger, minced

½ tsp ground cardamom seeds

½ tsp whole cloves

½ tsp red chili flakes

1½ tsp (4 g) kosher salt, divided

1½ cups (52 g) cubed, day-old firm white bread

1 cup (240 ml) whole milk

1 lb (455 g) ground lamb

1 egg, beaten

¼ tsp black pepper

⅛ tsp grated nutmeg

1 tsp ground ginger

1 tsp turmeric

2 tsp (5 g) paprika

¼ tsp cayenne pepper

¼ tsp ground cloves

¼ tsp ground coriander

½ tsp ground cumin

¼ cup (15 g) parsley, chopped, divided

3 tbsp (3 g) cilantro, chopped

3 tbsp (18 g) scallions, finely chopped

¼ cup (60 ml) grapeseed oil

Gyro Sliders with Tzatziki

Being raised in Astoria, New York—the most ethnically diverse city in America, according to National Geographic—I had the honor of experiencing authentic Greek food from the immigrants who once dominated the area. As a child, I recall experiencing the aromas of fresh charcoal-grilled souvlaki and gyros that would permeate the business district as I shopped with my parents. This recipe takes me back to that time.

Serves: 6

Sous vide cook time: 3 hours

Preheat the water bath to 150°F (65.5°C). In a food processor grind the lamb, beef, onion, parsley, cumin, marjoram, garlic, oregano, salt and pepper. Process the meat until it becomes a paste, using the spatula to scrape down the sides of the bowl as needed. Form the mixture into 6 slider patties and place on a parchment-lined sheet pan. Cover with plastic wrap and put in the freezer for 1 hour. When frozen, place the sliders into a bag, vacuum seal and place into the water bath. Cook for 3 hours.

Clean the food processor and drain the cucumbers (see Note) by folding them into a kitchen towel and twisting on both sides to squeeze out the excess water. Add the strained yogurt, drained cucumbers, lemon juice, garlic, dill, salt and pepper to the food processor and blend until smooth. Taste for seasoning, then refrigerate.

Remove the sliders from the water bath and pat dry with paper towels. Heat the oil in a pan over medium-high heat until smoking hot and sear each patty until browned, 2 to 3 minutes per side. Serve topped with tzatziki sauce on toasted slider buns.

> **Note:** Draining the cucumbers and using strained yogurt prevents the tzatziki sauce from becoming a watery mess.

Gyro

½ lb (225 g) ground lamb

½ lb (225 g) ground chuck beef, 20% fat

1 medium onion, chopped

¼ cup (15 g) fresh parsley

2 tsp (4 g) ground cumin

2 tsp (2 g) ground marjoram

3 cloves garlic, chopped

1 tsp ground oregano

1 tsp kosher salt

1 tsp ground pepper

3 tbsp (45 ml) grapeseed oil

6 slider buns, toasted

Tzatziki

2 medium cucumbers, seeded and finely chopped

16 oz (455 g) whole Greek yogurt, strained

Juice of 1 lemon

3 cloves garlic, chopped

1 tbsp (3 g) fresh dill, minced

½ tsp kosher salt

½ tsp black pepper

Classic Lobster Rolls

From as far north as the Canadian Maritime Islands and all the way down through the Mid-Atlantic region of the United States, succulent lobster presented in toasted buns is a seaside summertime treat. With this recipe, there is no reason to travel for this delicacy or to wait until summer.

Serves: 4

Sous vide cook time: 1 hour

Preheat the water bath to 140°F (60°C). Season the lobster tails with salt and pepper, then seal in a vacuum bag with 4 tablespoons (56 g) of cold butter. Place the bag in the water and cook for 1 hour.

While the lobster cooks, combine the celery, mayonnaise, lemon juice, 1 tablespoon (3 g) of parsley and tarragon in a bowl and whisk until fully incorporated, then cover and refrigerate it until the lobster is ready.

When it is ready, remove the lobster from the water and bag and allow it to cool for about 5 minutes. Cut the lobster tails into 1-inch (2.5-cm) pieces and fold them into the chilled mayonnaise mixture and refrigerate for at least 1 hour. Five minutes before serving, melt the 2 tablespoons (28 g) of remaining butter, then toast the buns and brush them with the melted butter. Top each bun with 6 ounces (170 g) of lobster meat and serve garnished with 1 tablespoon (3 g) of parsley and a side of Dill Pickles.

4 lobster tails, 6 oz (170 g) each

¼ tsp kosher salt

¼ tsp fresh black pepper

6 tbsp (85 g) unsalted butter, divided

1 large celery heart, finely chopped

½ cup (120 g) mayonnaise

3 tbsp (45 ml) fresh lemon juice

2 tbsp (6 g) flat-leaf parsley, finely chopped, divided

1 tbsp (3 g) tarragon, finely chopped

4 split-top buns or hot dog buns, toasted

Dill Pickles (page 180), for serving

Veal Tongue Tacos

Inexpensive, tough cuts of meat do particularly well in the sous vide. This marinated calf tongue is made fork-tender after nearly half a day in the water bath with spicy chipotles and New Mexico chili peppers.

Serves: 6 to 8

Sous vide cook time: 8 hours

Add the chipotle peppers, oregano, cumin, paprika and vinegar to a food processor and blend until smooth. Put the whole tongue into a bag and add the salt and the dried New Mexico pepper, if using, then pour in the chipotle mixture and vacuum seal. Refrigerate for 12 hours.

Heat the water bath to 190°F (87.7°C), lower the bagged tongue into the water and leave to cook for 8 hours. Carefully remove the bag from the water and allow the bag to cool slightly before opening. Remove the meat with a pair of tongs, discard the dried pepper and pour the remaining juices and the beef stock into a small saucepan over medium heat. Reduce the sauce until it thickens, about 8 to 10 minutes, then remove the saucepan from the heat and set aside.

Using a sharp knife, slice into the outer membrane of the tongue and peel the membrane away from the meat. This outer skin should slide off easily. Place the meat in a bowl and shred with two forks. Set up your tortillas and spoon the desired amount of meat on each. Top with lettuce, tomatoes, radish, jalapeño, queso fresco, cilantro and sour cream and serve with a dollop of the reserved pan sauce.

1 (14-oz [397-g]) can chipotle peppers in adobo sauce

1 tbsp (3 g) dried oregano

1 tbsp (7 g) ground cumin

1 tbsp (7 g) paprika

1 tbsp (15 ml) white vinegar

2 lbs (910 g) veal or beef tongue

½ tsp salt

1 large dried New Mexico chili pepper, optional

½ cup (120 ml) beef stock

12 soft corn or flour tortillas

1½ cups (108 g) shredded iceberg lettuce

2 plum tomatoes, seeded and finely chopped

2 small radishes, very thinly sliced on a mandoline

1 large jalapeño pepper, thinly sliced, optional

½ cup (60 g) queso fresco

1 cup (15 g) fresh cilantro, chopped

Sour cream, for serving

Sichuan Surf & Turf Meatballs

How do I make my pork meatballs even more moist and decadent, you ask? Add chopped oysters! Sichuan peppercorns, which are known for their spicy and numbing flavor, are paired with these bite-size morsels that are coated in a glossy, astringent and spicy sauce.

Serves: 4

Sous vide cook time: 2 hours

Preheat the water bath to 145°F (62.7°C). In a large bowl, add half of the minced garlic, half of the scallions, the ginger, pepper and egg whites. Whisk until combined, then gently fold in the pork, minced oysters and breadcrumbs. Form the mixture into 1½-inch (4-cm) meatballs and place on a parchment-lined baking sheet. Place the baking sheet in the freezer for 1½ to 2 hours. This will stiffen the meatballs so they won't be crushed during the vacuum process.

When frozen, place the meatballs into a bag, vacuum seal and place into the sous vide bath for 2 hours. Put 3 tablespoons (45 ml) of the oil into a saucepan over medium heat and stir in the remainder of the garlic, cooking for 30 to 45 seconds until it is fragrant. Add the chili bean paste, sherry, soy sauce, sugar and balsamic vinegar. Bring the mixture to a boil, stirring frequently, and cook until the sauce thickens, about 6 to 7 minutes. Cover and keep warm while you prepare the meatballs.

In a bowl, whisk the water and cornstarch until it is fully combined. Remove the meatballs from the bag and carefully dry with paper towels. In a wok, heat the remaining oil over high heat to 350°F (177°C). Dip each meatball into the cornstarch mixture and flash-fry them in batches until browned, about 1 to 2 minutes. Drain them on paper towels and drizzle with desired amount of sauce or serve the sauce separately for dipping. Garnish with half of the sliced scallions.

6 cloves garlic, minced, divided

2 scallions, thinly sliced, divided

1 tbsp (6 g) ginger, minced

15 Sichuan peppercorns, crushed finely in a mortar

2 egg whites

10 oz (285 g) ground pork

12 oysters, shucked and minced

¼ cup (30 g) plain breadcrumbs

3 cups (720 ml) canola oil, divided

¼ cup (57 g) red chili bean paste

2 tbsp (30 ml) dry sherry

2 tbsp (30 ml) low sodium soy sauce

2 tbsp (24 g) granulated sugar

1 tbsp (15 ml) balsamic vinegar

¼ cup (60 ml) water, optional

¼ cup (32 g) cornstarch, optional

Pulpo Gallego

Although these tender octopus tentacles in olive oil and herbs were popularized along the Northern Atlantic coast of Spain, they are eaten everywhere in the country. Here they are cooked perfectly in the sous vide bath.

Serves: 6 to 8

Sous vide cook time: 6 hours

Preheat the water bath to 171°F (77.2°C). Make an ice bath and bring a large pot of water to boil. Blanch the octopus in the boiling water, about 15 minutes. Remove it from the pot and immediately place it into the ice bath for 5 minutes. When the octopus is cool, season it with salt and place it in a vacuum bag with the olive oil and seal it. Cook for 6 hours.

Grease a grill with oil and set at high heat. Remove the octopus from the bag and place it onto the smoking hot grill. Cook the octopus, flipping it once, until you start to see charred bits on the legs, 3 to 5 minutes per side. Remove from the heat and allow it to cool slightly, then slice it into 1-inch (2.5-cm) pieces. Arrange the octopus on a platter with boiled potato cubes (if using) and sprinkle with paprika, more kosher salt and parsley, and drizzle with olive oil before serving.

1 whole octopus, 3½ lbs (1.6 kg), rinsed and beak removed

1 tbsp (8 g) kosher salt

¼ cup (60 ml) olive oil, plus more for drizzling

2 large potatoes, boiled and cubed, optional

2 tsp (5 g) smoked Spanish paprika

1 tbsp (3 g) fresh parsley

Olive oil, for serving

Fiery Harissa Shrimp

Inspired by the spicier dishes of Tunisia, this recipe can be served as a shared small plate with a cooling aioli or over couscous for a heartier meal. The spicy harissa paste, which is a blend of smoked chilis, garlic, mint, cumin and sometimes rose petals, is caramelized, whisked smooth with cold butter and tossed in a pan with sous vide—prepared shrimp.

Serves: 4 to 6
Sous vide cook time: 1 hour

Preheat the water bath to 140°F (60°C). Season the shrimp with salt and vacuum seal them in a single layer in a bag. Place the bag into the sous vide bath and cook for 1 hour.

Approximately 15 minutes before the shrimp are finished cooking, heat the oil in a nonstick skillet over medium-high heat. Spoon in the harissa paste and cook, stirring frequently, until it becomes slightly caramelized, 3 to 4 minutes. Add the garlic and cook until it becomes fragrant, 30 to 45 seconds. Lower the heat to low and stir in the cold butter, 1 tablespoon (14 g) at a time, until the mixture is smooth. Remove the pan from the heat and cover.

Take the vacuum bag out of the water bath, remove the shrimp and add them to the pan with the harissa sauce. Toss all together until the shrimp are coated, then sprinkle with the cilantro and serve immediately.

1½ lbs (680 g) large shrimp, tail on, shelled and deveined

½ tsp kosher salt

2 tbsp (30 ml) canola or grapeseed oil

½ cup (110 g) harissa paste

4 cloves garlic, minced

4 tbsp (56 g) cold unsalted butter

3 tbsp (3 g) fresh cilantro, chopped, for serving

Gochujang Cold Squid

The Korean-style sauce—which is sweet, spicy and salty—would usually be the highlight here, but this one is all about the cooking method. With the immersion circulator keeping the water at an even temperature, the squid has no chance of becoming rubbery.

Serves: 2 to 4

Sous vide cook time: 2 hours

Preheat the water bath to 138°F (58.8°C). Season the squid with salt and pepper, then place it in a bag and vacuum seal. Place the bag into the water and cook for 2 hours.

While the squid is cooking, make the sauce. In a bowl whisk together the chili paste, sesame oil, rice vinegar, soy sauce, garlic, ginger, pepper flakes and half of the scallions until everything is fully incorporated. Refrigerate until the squid is done cooking.

Remove the squid from the water and immerse it in an ice bath for 10 to 15 minutes. Cut the bag open, remove the squid and dry it on paper towels.

Heat a grill to high and brush the grates with oil. When the grates begin to smoke, use tongs to carefully lay the squid on the grill and cook 1 to 2 minutes per side. Set the squid aside to cool, then slice the body of the squid crosswise into ½-inch (13-mm) rings. In a large bowl toss the squid with the sauce, cover and refrigerate for 4 to 6 hours. Garnish with the remaining scallions and serve.

1 lb (455 g) squid, cleaned

1 tsp kosher salt

½ tsp black pepper

2 tbsp (30 g) Gochujang chili paste

1½ tbsp (22 ml) sesame oil

1 tbsp (15 ml) rice vinegar

2 tbsp (30 ml) soy sauce

2 cloves garlic, minced

2 tbsp (12 g) fresh ginger, minced

¼ tsp red pepper flakes

2 scallions, thinly sliced, divided

Chapter 7

beautiful brunches

Who doesn't love brunch? You can eat it almost any time you like and it's usually on the rich and filling side. At home, however, brunches are usually too elaborate for a weekday, and often best enjoyed with a group of friends or family members. The sous vide method takes the stress out of preparing these midmorning treats—even poached eggs for small or large gatherings. In this section are some of my favorite brunches.

Crab Cakes with Poached Eggs and Saffron Hollandaise

Talk to any chef about their kitchen headaches and odds are you'll hear "poached eggs" and "hollandaise." There is a simpler way to avoid common breakfast mishaps: sous vide! The rich egg yolks and zesty tang of the hollandaise sauce perfectly complement the oceanic flavor of the sweet crabmeat.

Serves: 6 to 8
Sous vide cook time: 50 minutes

In a large bowl gently mix the crab, crushed crackers, bell pepper, scallions, jalapeño (if using) and parsley together until evenly combined. In a separate small bowl, whisk together the eggs, mayonnaise, Dijon, Worcestershire, lemon juice, hot sauce and Old Bay seasoning until the ingredients are well blended. Using your hands, gently fold the wet ingredients into the crab mixture until you have the desired consistency. Remember to handle the mixture gently so as not to break up the crab too much. Form the crab cakes into 6 to 8 patties, then place them on a plate, cover and refrigerate for 1 to 3 hours to allow the patties to firm up. While the patties are chilling, prepare the Saffron Hollandaise according to the directions on page 175 and begin preparing the eggs.

Preheat the water bath to 145°F (63°C). About 1 hour into the hollandaise cooking time, put the eggs into a ziplock bag (or pasta basket) to keep the eggs somewhat immobile while the water circulates, and slowly lower the eggs into the sous vide bath for 50 minutes. About 30 minutes into the cook time for the eggs, heat a medium pan of water over medium-low heat until it is barely simmering—do not allow it to boil.

Preheat the oven to 350°F (177°C). Fifteen minutes before the eggs and sauce are ready, remove the crab cakes from the refrigerator. Lightly dust them with the flour, shaking off any excess. Heat a cast-iron pan over medium-high heat, then add the grapeseed oil. When the oil is hot, lay the crab cakes in the pan and brown one side, approximately 4 to 5 minutes. When they are ready to flip, do so gently and then place the pan directly into the hot oven for 10 to 15 minutes. Remove the crab cakes, cover and keep warm while the eggs cook.

Remove the eggs from the sous vide and use a spoon to gently crack the eggs over the barely simmering pot of water that has been on standby. Let them slip carefully into the water and leave them there for 30 seconds (see Note). Remove the eggs with a slotted spoon, leaving the "loose whites" behind. Place a crab cake on top of each English muffin half, then top with the poached eggs and hollandaise and garnish with fish roe or sea salt flakes.

Note: For a faster poached egg you can set the temperature to 167°F (75°C) and cook for 11 minutes.

1 lb (455 g) canned lump crabmeat

2 oz (57 g) saltine crackers, finely crushed (about 20 crackers)

2 tbsp (14 g) red bell pepper, minced

3 tbsp (18 g) scallions, thinly sliced

1 tbsp (7 g) minced jalapeño, optional

2 tbsp (6 g) parsley, finely chopped

2 small eggs, beaten

½ cup (120 g) mayonnaise

1 tbsp (13 g) Dijon mustard

1 tbsp (15 ml) Worcestershire sauce

1 tbsp (15 ml) lemon juice

2 tsp (10 ml) hot sauce

1 tbsp (8 g) Old Bay seasoning

Saffron Hollandaise (page 175)

8 large eggs, in the shell

Flour, for dusting

¼ cup (60 ml) grapeseed oil

4 English muffins, split and toasted

Fish roe, for garnish, optional

Sea salt flakes to finish, for garnish, optional

Mexican Brunch Burger

This tasty, belly-busting breakfast burger has all the flavors from south of the border! This dish is perfect for when you can't decide between breakfast and lunch. The smoky flavors of chipotle and paprika are balanced by the queso and crema in this mouthwatering burger.

Serves: 4
Sous vide cook time: 1½ hours

Preheat the water bath to 134°F (56.6°C). In a small bowl whisk together the coriander, cumin, paprika, ancho powder, chipotle powder, salt and pepper until fully combined.

In a large mixing bowl, add the ground beef, sprinkle the seasoning mix into it and knead the mixture with your hands until combined. Mold the beef into four 6-ounce (170-g) patties and place them in a vacuum bag in a single layer. Seal, then place into the sous vide bath and cook for 1½ hours. Remove the burgers from the bag and pat dry with paper towels.

Spread the crema on the toasted English muffins or buns. Heat the grapeseed oil in a cast-iron pan over high heat until it is smoking. Brown the burgers in the pan, 2 to 3 minutes per side, and remove each to a toasted English muffin or hamburger bun. Top each burger with sliced avocado, 2 ounces (58 g) queso fresco, 1 tablespoon (8 g) Pickled Red Onions, 1 fried egg and cilantro and serve.

1 tsp coriander

1 tsp cumin

1 tsp smoked paprika

1 tsp ancho chili powder

1 tsp chipotle chili powder

1 tsp kosher salt

1 tsp black pepper

1½ lbs (680 g) ground beef

½ cup (100 g) Mexican crema or sour cream

4 toasted English muffins or hamburger buns

2 tbsp (30 ml) grapeseed oil

1 avocado, quartered and thinly sliced

8 oz (225 g) queso fresco, divided

¼ cup (33 g) Pickled Red Onions (page 179), optional

4 small eggs, fried

¼ cup (4 g) cilantro, roughly chopped

Crustless Quiche Lorraine

With both Gruyère and Raclette, this quiche has all the comforts of a traditional French egg and vegetable tart, but with an Alpine emphasis on true Swiss cheeses.

Serves: 6
Sous vide cook time: 1½ hours

Preheat the water bath to 170°F (76.6°C). Melt the butter in a skillet over medium-high heat and add the bacon, shallots, bay leaf and thyme. Stir occasionally until the butter starts to bubble. Reduce the heat to low and cook, stirring occasionally, until the bacon is cooked through, 15 to 20 minutes. Remove the skillet from the heat and allow the bacon mixture to cool.

Puree the eggs with an immersion blender on high speed until they become foamy, then add the half and half, cayenne, nutmeg, salt and pepper. Puree again until smooth.

When the bacon has cooled, place an even amount of the bacon mixture into six half-pint (237-ml) Mason jars. Fill the jars with an equal amount of the egg mixture, leaving ¾ inch (2 cm) of space for topping with grated cheese. Sprinkle the Gruyère and Raclette cheeses evenly on top of the eggs in each jar, being sure not to fill to the absolute top. As a rule of thumb, you should have about ½ inch (13 mm) of space between the contents of your jar and the top of the jar.

Seal the jar (see Sous Vide Basics on page 11) and cook for 1½ hours in the water bath, making sure there is at least 1 inch (2.5 cm) of water above the tops of the jars. At the end of the cooking time, carefully remove the jars with silicone tongs and place on a heat-safe surface to cool for 30 minutes before serving or refrigerating. The quiches can be kept refrigerated for up to 3 days and can be reheated in a water bath at 170°F (76.6°C) for 10 minutes.

3 tbsp (42 g) unsalted butter

6 oz (170 g) bacon, cut into ¼-inch (6-mm) pieces

2 shallots, thinly sliced

1 bay leaf

2 sprigs fresh thyme, finely chopped

10 eggs

1¼ cups (300 ml) half and half

¼ tsp cayenne pepper

½ tsp nutmeg

2 tsp (10 g) salt

½ tsp black pepper

4 oz (115 g) grated Gruyère

4 oz (115 g) grated Raclette

Hawaiian Loco Moco

Asian and American influences flavor this hearty Hawaiian breakfast. I came across this dish during a trip to Hawaii and found the idea of a burger with rice, savory gravy and a sunny-side egg was a peculiar first meal of the day. Breakfast for me has never been the same since!

Serves: 4
Sous vide cook time: 1 hour

Preheat the water bath to 134°F (56.6°C). Season the beef patties with salt and pepper, then place them into a vacuum bag and seal. Place the sealed patties into the sous vide bath and cook for 1 hour.

While the burgers are cooking, heat the olive oil in a sauté pan over medium-high heat. Add the onion and mushrooms to the pan and cook, stirring occasionally, until the onion is translucent, soft and beginning to brown, 10 to 12 minutes. Remove the mixture to a bowl and set aside.

Cook the rice according to directions on the packaging, cover and keep warm.

Melt the butter in a sauté pan over medium-high heat and whisk in the flour until it is fully incorporated. Lower the heat slightly and continue whisking until the roux becomes light brown in color, 8 to 10 minutes. Then stir in the mirin, soy sauce and beef stock. Cook the mixture until it reduces by half and thickens a bit, about 15 minutes. Add the onions and mushrooms into the gravy, cover and set aside.

Lightly coat grill grates with oil. Remove the beef patties from the bag, pat dry with paper towels and place them on the grill over high heat. Brown the beef on the grill for about 2 minutes per side, then transfer to a plate and keep warm.

Fry the eggs sunny-side up (soft yolks recommended, but not necessary). Divide the rice among four plates, top each with a burger, then spoon the onion and mushroom gravy across the patty, top with a fried egg, garnish with scallions and serve.

1½ lbs (680 g) ground chuck beef, formed into four 6-oz (170-g) patties

Kosher salt

Black pepper

2 tbsp (30 ml) olive oil

1 large onion, thinly sliced

5 oz (142 g) shiitake mushrooms, sliced

4 cups (645 g) cooked white rice

3 tbsp (42 g) butter, unsalted

3 tbsp (24 g) all-purpose flour

1 tbsp (15 ml) mirin

2 tbsp (30 ml) soy sauce

2 cups (480 ml) low sodium beef stock

4 large eggs

2 scallions, thinly sliced, for garnish

Chapter 8

vivid
vegetable sides

One of the benefits of cooking vegetables with the sous vide method is that the important vitamins and minerals are not lost during the cooking process, as can happen with direct high heat cooking such as boiling or roasting. The vegetables also maintain their color and vibrancy on their way to your plate.

Honey-Glazed Heirloom Carrots

Rainbow carrots add colorful nutrition to any meal. Whether you serve them for the holidays or eat them all year round, glazed carrots are a favorite. When slow cooked in the sous vide bath at a precise temperature then sautéed in butter and honey, these carrots will have your dinner guests screaming for more!

Serves: 4 to 6

Sous vide cook time: 1 hour

Preheat the water bath to 183°F (83.8°C). Separate the carrots by color and place each batch in its own vacuum bag. This will prevent the colors of darker carrots from bleeding onto the lighter colored carrots. Add 1 sprig of thyme and 1 tablespoon (14 g) of butter to each bag, vacuum seal them and place into the water bath for 1 hour. If you are using an ice bath to save the carrots for a later time (see Note), prepare the ice bath 5 minutes before the carrots are due to be removed from the sous vide bath.

Remove the carrots from the bags and heat the remaining 2 tablespoons (28 g) of butter in a sauté pan over medium-high heat. When the butter has melted and is foaming, add the honey and stir for 30 seconds. Add the lemon juice and carrots to the pan, then toss them until they are fully coated with the honey mixture. Season with salt and pepper and serve garnished with the fresh parsley.

Note: The bagged carrots can be dropped into an ice bath and refrigerated for up to 3 days then reheated in a pan. If plain carrots are desired, simply sauté them in a pan with only butter and serve.

2 bunches (about 2 lbs [910 g]) baby rainbow carrots, peeled and stemmed

4 sprigs thyme

6 tbsp (85 g) unsalted butter, divided

4 tbsp (60 ml) honey

2 tbsp (30 ml) lemon juice

Kosher salt

Black pepper

¼ cup (15 g) parsley, finely chopped, for garnish

Vinegar and Herb Potato Salad

This warm vinegar-based potato salad is a perfect side dish for your backyard BBQ or weeknight family dinner.

Serves: 6

Sous vide cook time: 1 hour

Preheat the water bath to 194°F (90°C). Add the red wine vinegar, ¾ cup (180 ml) olive oil, oregano, rosemary and garlic to a bowl and process with an immersion blender for 30 to 45 seconds. Stir in the chopped red onion and parsley, then cover and keep at room temperature.

Season the cubed potatoes with salt and pepper. Add 1 tablespoon (15 ml) of olive oil to each of the two vacuum bags. Divide the potatoes in half and place an even amount in each bag in a single layer to ensure even cooking. Vacuum seal and cook for 1 hour.

Remove the potatoes from the bags and place an even amount on each plate. Spoon the herbed dressing over the potatoes and serve.

½ cup (120 ml) red wine vinegar

¾ cup (180 ml) plus 2 tbsp (30 ml) olive oil, divided

¼ cup (10 g) fresh oregano, chopped

1 sprig rosemary, finely chopped

1 clove garlic, chopped

1 large red onion, finely chopped

¼ cup (15 g) fresh parsley, chopped

3 lbs (1.4 kg) red potatoes, scrubbed and cut into 1-inch (2.5-cm) cubes

Kosher salt

Black pepper

Butter and Garlic Asparagus

This flavorful and garlicky asparagus is cooked to perfection in the water bath, while maintaining its bright color and "snap."

Serves: 6

Sous vide cook time: 12 minutes

Preheat the water bath to 180°F (82.2°C). Place the asparagus in a large vacuum bag in a single layer. Add the butter, garlic and lemon juice to the bag and vacuum seal. Place it into the water bath and cook for 12 minutes.

Remove the bag and, if meant for later use, plunge the bag into an ice bath (see Note). If serving immediately, plate the asparagus, season with salt and pepper and drizzle with olive oil.

Note: After shocking the asparagus in the ice bath, it can be refrigerated up to 3 days.

2 lbs (910 g) asparagus, tough stems trimmed from the bottom

4 tbsp (56 g) unsalted butter

2 cloves garlic, crushed

2 tbsp (30 ml) lemon juice

Kosher salt

Black pepper

Olive oil, for drizzling, optional

Caramelized Cabbage Wedges

When I was growing up, eating boiled or stir-fried cabbage was the norm in our household. Cooking the cabbage wedges sous vide helps this standard side maintain flavor and a firm tenderness.

Serves: 4

Sous vide cook time: 4 hours

Preheat the water bath to 183°F (83.8°C). Put the roasted garlic paste, thyme, water and cabbage in a vacuum bag and seal. Place it into the water bath and cook for 4 hours, then remove it and allow the bag to cool for 10 to 15 minutes.

Carefully remove the cabbage wedges from the bag so they retain their wedge shape and discard the rest of the contents. Heat the butter in a nonstick pan over medium-high heat until the butter is foaming. Season the wedges with salt and black pepper and place them cut-side down into the pan. Cook the wedges, without moving them, 3 to 4 minutes per side until brown and caramelized. Remove the cabbage to four plates and serve.

2 tsp (6 g) roasted garlic paste, divided

2 sprigs thyme

2 tbsp (30 ml) water

2½-lb (1.13-kg) head of green cabbage, cut into wedges

3 tbsp (42 g) unsalted butter

Kosher salt

Black pepper

Buttery Root Vegetables

This recipe is inspired by traditional rotmos, a Scandinavian comfort food of mashed rutabaga, sometimes with carrots, sometimes without. Here is my take on warm, comforting root vegetables that can be the perfect side paired with any protein entrée in this book, but particularly with Dill Salmon (page 111). I leave my vegetables in this dish as is when they come out of the sous vide bath, but you can mash them if you'd like.

Serves: 6
Sous vide cook time: 3 hours

Preheat the water bath to 185°F (85°C). Season the rutabaga, parsnips and carrots with the salt, pepper and nutmeg. Place the rutabaga, carrots, parsnips, roasted garlic, thyme and butter into a vacuum bag and seal. Place the bag into the sous vide bath and cook for 3 hours.

When the vegetables are done, remove them from the bag and strain the liquid into a sauté pan over medium-high heat. When the mixture is hot, add the vegetables and sauté until slightly caramelized, about 5 to 10 minutes. Remove from the heat, allow to cool and serve.

1 lb (455 g) rutabaga, peeled and cut into 1-inch (2.5-cm) pieces

12 oz (340 g) parsnips, peeled and cut into 1-inch (2.5-cm) pieces

½ lb (225 g) carrots, peeled and cut into 1-inch (2.5-cm) pieces

Kosher salt

Black pepper

1 tsp nutmeg

8–10 cloves garlic, roasted

2 sprigs thyme

1 cup (230 g) unsalted butter

Garlic Mashed Potatoes

You want rich, creamy potatoes? Try cooking your spuds sous vide style. You will never need to worry about water-saturated potatoes again.

Serves: 4

Sous vide cook time: 45 minutes

Preheat the water bath to 194°F (90°C). Add the sliced potatoes, thyme, butter, roasted garlic and heavy cream into a vacuum bag and seal it. Place it into the sous vide bath and cook for 45 minutes.

Remove the bag from the sous vide bath, cut open one side and strain the liquid into a bowl. Discard the thyme sprig. Process the potatoes and roasted garlic with a food mill or potato masher until they are fully smashed, then stir in the reserved liquid until smooth. Season with salt and pepper to taste and serve garnished with chopped chives.

2 lbs (910 g) russet potatoes, sliced into ½-inch (13-mm) thick rounds

1 sprig thyme, optional

8 tbsp (115 g) unsalted butter

8 cloves roasted garlic

¾ cup (180 ml) heavy cream

Kosher salt

Black pepper

Chopped chives, for garnish

Chapter 9

delectable desserts

I'll admit, desserts were never my specialty, mostly because I never could call myself a baker. But once I started experimenting with sous vide desserts, all of my sweet dreams came true! Some of these recipes call for cooking in canning jars, which allow you to prepare cheesecakes and puddings preportioned in single-serving jars. If you have children, expect them to line up at the kitchen after dinner.

Cardamom-Spiced Pears in Red Wine

The combination of bold winter spices and full-bodied red wine reduction creates a simple yet visually stunning and delicious dessert. When served warm, the flavors of nutmeg, allspice and cardamom will give you a comforting holiday-like feeling.

Serves: 8

Sous vide cook time: 1 hour 15 minutes

Preheat the water bath to 175°F (79.4°C). Pour the wine and sugar into a medium saucepan and stir until the sugar dissolves. Stir in the cardamom, orange zest, cinnamon stick, star anise, cloves, allspice, nutmeg and vanilla bean. Bring the mixture to a rolling boil, then reduce the heat and simmer until the wine reduces by nearly half, about 25 to 30 minutes. Remove from the heat, strain the mixture through a sieve into a bowl and discard the solids.

If you are using a chamber sealer, place the pears into a vacuum bag in a single layer, pour the wine mixture into the bag and seal it on a gentle setting to avoid crushing the pears. If you are using the water displacement method, put the pears in a freezer bag, pour in the wine, then submerge it in the water bath. Use a kitchen clip to secure the bag to the container to minimize bag movement during cooking. Cook for 1 hour and 15 minutes.

Remove the bag from the water. If you wish to serve the pears cold, submerge the sealed bag into an ice bath for 15 to 20 minutes and refrigerate the entire bag until ready to use. If serving the pears warm, allow them to cool down a bit before plating. Pour 2 tablespoons (30 ml) of the bagged liquid into eight individual bowls. Place a pear half in each bowl and add whipped cream or a scoop of ice cream. Garnish with a mint sprig and serve.

Note: Chilled pears can be reheated with the sous vide at 150°F (65.5°C) for 30 minutes.

1 (25-oz [750-ml]) bottle full-bodied red wine, such as cabernet sauvignon or merlot

2½ cups (500 g) white sugar

6 cardamom pods

1 tbsp (9 g) orange zest

1 cinnamon stick

1 star anise

3 whole cloves

½ tsp allspice

½ tsp nutmeg

1 vanilla bean, split

4 Bosc or Anjou pears, peeled, cored and halved

Whipped cream or ice cream, for serving

Fresh mint sprigs, for garnish

Berry Cheesecake

Cheesecake can be a very decadent dessert, but when it's topped with a sweet and tart berry sauce, it ramps it up to a whole new level! Using Mason jars in a gentle water bath makes the whole process so easy.

Serves: 5
Sous vide cook time: 90 minutes

Preheat the water bath to 176°F (80°C) while you prepare the batter and crust. Preheat the oven to 350°F (177°C). Melt the butter in a medium skillet over low heat, then add in the sugar and stir until the sugar is dissolved into the butter. Remove the butter mixture from the heat and add the graham cracker or vanilla wafer crumbs, tossing until well coated. Spread the crumbs evenly across the bottom of the skillet, then place it in the oven. The crumbs will become toasted in about 10 minutes; keep checking to avoid burning. Remove the skillet from the oven, transfer the crumb mixture onto a cool plate and set aside.

Place the softened cream cheese, sugar and salt in a food processor and blend until smooth, stopping occasionally to use the spatula to scrape down the sides of the blender bowl. Add the eggs and the vanilla extract to the mixture and blend until smooth, then add the heavy cream and blend another 2 minutes, making sure no lumps remain.

Spoon 1½ tablespoons (11 g) of cooled graham cracker crumbs into the bottom of each Mason jar, making sure to spread it evenly. Fill each jar slowly with approximately 4 ounces (115 ml) of batter, leaving enough space for your berry topping. Seal the jars (see Sous Vide Basics, page 11) and, using canning tongs, carefully lower the jars into the water. They are sealed properly if you see a few small bubbles escape the jars. Cook for 90 minutes. While this happens, prepare the sauce.

In a saucepan over medium heat, stir together the frozen raspberries, the sugar and ½ cup (120 ml) of water until the sugar is dissolved. Increase the heat to medium-high and bring the mixture to a boil, stirring often, then reduce the heat and add the vanilla. In a small bowl, combine the cornstarch and 2 tablespoons (30 ml) of water and whisk until incorporated. Pour the cornstarch slurry into the hot raspberry mixture and bring it back to a boil. Stir and boil over medium-low heat for 4 minutes or until the mixture has thickened a bit. Strain the mixture through a sieve into a bowl to remove the seeds. Pour the sauce back into the pan, add the diced strawberries and simmer for 5 minutes until the strawberries soften. Remove from the heat and add the butter, stirring until it melts. Allow the mixture to cool for 20 to 30 minutes.

Using canning tongs, remove the cheesecakes from the water and set on the counter until they cool, about 30 minutes. Open each jar and top the cheesecake with 2 tablespoons (30 ml) of the cooled berry mixture, seal tightly and place in the refrigerator overnight or for at least 8 hours before serving.

Cracker Crust

2 tbsp (28 g) butter

2 tsp (8 g) sugar

½ cup (42 g) graham cracker or vanilla wafer crumbs, crushed

Cheese Filling

16 oz (455 g) cream cheese, softened

½ cup (100 g) white sugar

⅛ tsp salt

3 large eggs

½ tsp vanilla extract

½ cup (120 ml) heavy cream

Berry Sauce

12 oz (340 g) frozen unsweetened raspberries

¾ cup (150 g) granulated sugar

½ cup (120 ml) plus 2 tbsp (30 ml) water, divided

½ tsp vanilla extract

2 tsp (5 g) cornstarch

2 tbsp (30 ml) water

3–4 fresh strawberries, diced

1 tbsp (14 g) unsalted butter

Nutty Crème Brûlée

Translated from the French as "burnt cream," this rich custard dessert with a light nutty almond or hazelnut flavor and crisp caramel topping will have your guests lining up for seconds.

Serves: 5

Sous vide cook time: 1 hour

Preheat the water bath to 176°F (80°C). Whisk together the egg yolks, 6 tablespoons (72 g) of sugar, almond extract and salt in a large bowl until smooth. Add the cream and continue whisking until fully incorporated and smooth. Strain the mixture through a sieve to remove air bubbles. Using a measuring cup with a spout, slowly pour 5½ ounces (160 ml) of the mixture into each of the five jars. Allow the jars to sit for 30 minutes so that any bubbles present will rise to the surface.

Using your kitchen torch, quickly flash the surface of each custard with a high flame, which will cause any bubbles to pop. Do not allow the flame to linger directly on the surface or you will scorch it. When you are satisfied that the bubbles have been eliminated, seal the jars (see Sous Vide Basics, page 11).

Using tongs, place the jars in the water bath and cook for 1 hour. Remove the jars from the water and allow to cool on a heat-safe surface for 20 minutes. Prepare an ice bath and submerge the jars in the ice bath to chill completely before you refrigerate the crème brûlées for at least 1 hour and up to 1 week before serving.

To serve, remove the jars from the refrigerator 30 minutes before conducting the final steps. Open the jars and, using the remaining tablespoon (12 g) of sugar, spread an even, thin layer of sugar over the custards. Using a kitchen torch, caramelize the sugar by moving the torch in circular motions 3 to 5 inches (8 to 13 cm) above the jars. Move the flame swiftly while moving closer and farther from the sugar until you have melted and browned the tops. Allow the crème brûlées to rest at least 5 minutes before serving. The sugar on top should be hard and crackly.

11 egg yolks
7 tbsp (84 g) white sugar, divided
1 tsp almond or hazelnut extract
Pinch of salt
21 oz (620 ml) heavy cream

Banana Pudding Pie with Rum-Infused Whipped Cream

I've never met a kid who doesn't like banana pudding, especially with vanilla wafers for dipping. I'm no kid, but I still adore this dessert, made all the more adult here with an infusion of rum whipped cream.

Serves: 5

Sous vide cook time: 1 hour

Preheat the water bath to 176°F (80°C) and place an empty whipped cream dispenser, with the top off, into the refrigerator (see Note). In a small mixing bowl, combine 1 tablespoon (12 g) of sugar and the cornstarch and mix until combined. In a large bowl whisk the egg yolks, salt and remaining 5 tablespoons (60 g) of sugar until smooth and set aside. In a large saucepan over medium-high heat, bring the milk, light cream and the sugar–cornstarch mixture to a boil. Reduce the heat to medium and simmer, stirring frequently, until the mixture slightly thickens. Remove the mixture from the heat and very slowly drizzle the warm milk into the egg mixture a little at a time, pausing to whisk it after adding every couple of tablespoons, until the egg mixture is tempered and fully incorporated. Whisk the banana extract into the mixture and strain the liquid through a sieve into a bowl. Allow it to rest for 20 to 30 minutes.

Use a small spoon to skim off any bubbles that form on the surface of the mixture. Add about 2 tablespoons (15 g) of the Cracker Crust (page 166) to the bottom of each of the canning jars (saving some to sprinkle on top). Slowly pour an equal amount of the pudding mixture into each of the five jars, leaving ¾ inch (2 cm) of space at the top. Seal the jar (see Sous Vide Basics, page 11) and carefully place them into the water bath with kitchen tongs. Cook for 1 hour.

While the pudding cooks, remove the whipped cream dispenser from the refrigerator and prepare the whipped cream. Place the powdered sugar, heavy cream, rum and vanilla extract into the siphon and shake well. Charge it with two N2O cartridges, shake it well once more and refrigerate.

Carefully remove the jars from the water bath and set them on a heat-safe surface to cool for 30 to 35 minutes. Seal the jars tight and refrigerate for at least 6 to 8 hours. Serve with banana slices, leftover wafer crumbles and rum-infused whipped cream.

6 tbsp (72 g) granulated sugar, divided

2 tbsp (15 g) cornstarch

8 egg yolks

1 tsp salt

14 oz (415 ml) whole milk

5½ oz (160 ml) light cream

1 tsp banana extract

Cracker Crust (page 166)

¼ cup (25 g) powdered sugar

1 pint (475 ml) heavy cream

2 tbsp (30 ml) light rum

½ tsp vanilla extract

1 thinly sliced banana, for serving, optional

Note: A "whipping siphon" is a canister that uses nitrous oxide charges that turns cream into whipped cream. Placing it into the refrigerator ahead of time allows the canister to cool before adding the cold cream.

classic condiments

You don't need a refrigerator full of store-bought jars or a pantry stacked with cans to have a few great condiments on hand. Just whip them up yourself with your sous vide device and some good quality storage items like Mason jars and a set of silicone tongs for safety. From a few classic French sauces to simple pickling methods to a sweet topping, keep these recipes handy to enhance your everyday meals.

Saffron Hollandaise

You'll be hard-pressed to find someone who isn't impressed by a smooth, creamy hollandaise. The saffron intensifies the overall experience and the sous vide method is nearly foolproof. Use it to top Crab Cakes with Poached Eggs (page 141) or your next steamed lobster dish.

Yield: About 1 cup (230 g)

Sous vide cook time: 1 hour

Preheat the water bath to 145°F (62.7°C). In a small saucepan over medium-high heat, cook the vinegar and shallots until the vinegar reduces to about 2 tablespoons (30 ml) and becomes syrupy, 8 to 10 minutes, then remove from the heat. Using a sieve or cheesecloth, strain the liquid into a ziplock bag. Add the eggs, butter, lemon juice and saffron threads to the bag. Vacuum seal the bag (or use the water displacement method) and lower it into the water bath for 1 hour.

Remove from the water bath and pour the contents into a blender, add the salt and pepper to taste and blend until the mixture is smooth. If the sauce is a little thin, you can cover it and set aside for about 5 to 7 minutes while you prepare the rest of your meal, and it should thicken a bit more as it sits. Any sauce not used right away can be placed into a bag or half-pint (237-ml) Mason jar and kept warm in the water bath for up to 1 hour.

2 oz (60 ml) champagne vinegar

3 tbsp (30 g) shallots, minced

4 large egg yolks, beaten

11 tbsp (154 g) unsalted butter

1 tbsp (15 ml) lemon juice

¼ tsp saffron threads

Kosher salt

White pepper

Note: This sauce does not save well, so it is best to use it the same day you make it.

Béarnaise Sauce

Tangy, herbaceous and oh so French, a béarnaise sauce—one of the five mother sauces of classic French cooking—will elevate your Veal Oscar (page 37) or top those weekend grilled steaks and burgers.

Yield: 1⅓ cups (320 ml)

Sous vide cook time: 45 minutes

Preheat the water bath to 145°F (62.7°C). In a small saucepan over medium-high heat, bring 1 tablespoon (2.5 g) of the tarragon, the shallots, vinegar, white wine and peppercorns to a boil, then lower the heat and simmer until reduced to about 4 tablespoons (60 ml) (the mixture should be syrupy), 8 to 10 minutes. Remove from the heat, strain the liquid through a sieve and set it aside to cool.

Whisk the egg yolks in a separate bowl until smooth. In a ziplock bag add the butter, strained reduction and egg yolks and use the water displacement method to place it into the sous vide bath. Cook for 45 minutes.

Remove the bag from the water and dump its contents into a bowl. Process the mixture with an immersion blender until it thickens. Taste and add salt and white pepper as needed. Stir in the remaining 1 tablespoon (2.5 g) of tarragon and serve. Alternatively, the sauce can be placed into a bag or half-pint, (237-ml) Mason jar and kept warm in the water bath for up to 1 hour.

2 tbsp (5 g) fresh tarragon, finely chopped, divided

2 medium shallots, minced

½ cup (120 ml) champagne vinegar

½ cup (120 ml) dry white wine

6–8 whole black peppercorns

2½ oz (74 g) egg yolks (about 4)

1⅓ cups (300 g) butter, unsalted

Kosher salt

White pepper

Note: This sauce does not save well, so it is best to use it the same day you make it.

Pickled Red Onions

Once you see how simple it is to make your own pickled onions in the sous vide, you'll wish you had started your pickling career sooner. They're just as at home on a Mexican Brunch Burger (page 142) as on the Cumin-Spiced Lamb Burger (page 89) or as an accompaniment to Pernil (page 70).

Yield: 2 cups (300 g)
Sous vide cook time: 2½ hours

Preheat the water bath to 140°F (60°C). Whisk together the white wine vinegar, water, sugar and salt until the sugar and salt are dissolved. Place the onions in the canning jars, 1 onion per jar, being careful not to fill to the top. Pour an equal amount of the brine over the onions until completely covered, leaving at least ½ inch (13 mm) to the top of the jar. As a rule of thumb, you always want to keep ½ inch (13 mm) between the top of the contents and the top of the jar. Seal the jar (see Sous Vide Basics, page 11) and place into the sous vide bath for 2½ hours. Remove the jars to a heat-safe surface and allow them to cool to room temperature. Onions can be stored in a cool, dark place for up to 6 months.

1½ cups (360 ml) white wine vinegar

1½ cups (360 ml) water

5 tbsp (60 g) granulated sugar

3 tbsp (54 g) salt

2 large red onions, thinly sliced on a mandoline, divided

Dill Pickles

What's the use of a pickling recipe without a traditional cucumber pickle? I'm partial to dill and Kosher pickles myself. Serve with any of the sandwiches in this book, but especially sliced onto the Miami Cubano Sandwich (page 73).

Yield: 8 to 10 pickles

Sous vide cook time: 2½ hours

Preheat the water bath to 140°F (60°C). Whisk together the white wine vinegar, water, sugar and salt until the sugar and salt are dissolved. Place 8 to 10 cucumbers, the dill sprigs, garlic and pepper flakes in a canning jar, being careful not to fill to the top. Pour the brine over the cucumbers until completely covered, leaving at least ½ inch (13 mm) of space to the top of the jar. As a rule of thumb, you always want to keep ½ inch (13 mm) of space between the top of the contents and the top of the jar. Seal the jar (see Sous Vide Basics, page 11) and place it into the sous vide bath for 2½ hours. Remove the jars to a heat-safe surface and allow the jar to cool to room temperature. Pickles can be stored in a cool, dark place for up to 6 months.

1½ cups (360 ml) white wine vinegar

1½ cups (360 ml) water

5 tbsp (60 g) granulated sugar

1½ tbsp (27 g) salt

8–10 baby cucumbers, quartered

4 sprigs fresh dill

2 cloves garlic, minced

1 tsp red pepper flakes

Dulce de Leche

Literally "sweet milk," dulce de leche is an incredibly popular caramel sauce made throughout Latin America and enjoyed on cakes, puddings and—let's be honest—even straight off a spoon.

Serves: 12 to 14

Sous vide cook time: 13 hours

Preheat the water bath to 185°F (85°C). Pour the condensed milk into a canning jar and seal the jar (see Sous Vide Basics, page 11). With silicone tongs, place the jar into the water bath. After 13 hours, carefully remove the jar and leave it to cool on a heat-safe surface. If serving the dulce de leche warm, allow it to cool slightly before drizzling on the dessert of your choice. Once the jar is at room temperature, you can refrigerate the topping for up to 2 weeks.

1 (14-oz [414-ml]) can of sweetened condensed milk

Ice cream or other dessert of your choosing, for serving

Note: Never put hot jars into the fridge or in ice water until they cool, or you risk cracking the jars.

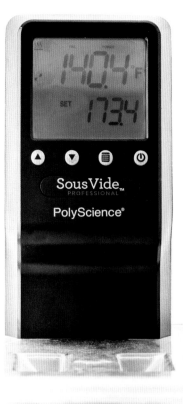

essential equipment

Broiler, kitchen torch or grill

Broilers are one viable alternative to browning meats after they are removed from the sous vide bath, but there is also a risk of overcooking food if broiling is not done carefully. If you do not have access to a broiler, a handheld kitchen torch can work well in a pinch. Meanwhile, some kitchen torches can give your food an off-putting taste and odor of gas. Recently, I discovered a solution to eliminating the gas flavor when using a torch, a one-of-a-kind attachment available for kitchen torches called Searzall®. This attachment takes the direct flame of the torch and spreads it out, giving you a handheld broiler. I find it a great option because you can control the browning of your food without cooking it any further than what the sous vide has already done. Indoor or outdoor grills are great as well for giving food that extra finished flavor. Throughout the book, you'll find recommendations on searing tools specific to each recipe.

Cast-iron or heavy-bottomed skillet

Heavy-bottom skillets are necessary for searing and browning foods either before sealing and cooking, or after they are removed from the sous vide bath. At the point of removal from the sous vide bath, the meat you prepared may not look appetizing; that is where your skillet comes in. Browning meats is the one thing that cannot be produced with the sous vide device alone. Accomplishing this requires the Maillard reaction to take place. This process happens when a protein has all of its surface moisture dried and comes in direct contact with a heat source of at least 310°F (155°C). The sugars react with the proteins and amino acids, which causes the meat to turn color. The caramelization that takes place adds a ton of flavor as well as the browning that is commonly seen when using traditional cooking methods.

The Searzall torch attachment lets you control the browning process.

Cast-iron skillets and indoor grills are necessary for searing.

Heatproof jars work well in the sous vide bath.

Cooking racks or weights

Depending on what you are cooking, you will need to consider weighing down the vacuum pouches so they stay fully submerged. There are sous vide racks available on a few websites. These racks help keep your items submerged in the water bath and your bags organized. If you don't have a rack, any heatproof kitchen weight will work (even a heavy pot lid or steamer basket can stand in).

Heatproof cooking vessel

There are quite a few things I have used as a container to cook in: a large stockpot, a polycarbonate sous vide container or even a cooler. The important thing is that your vessel of choice is large enough to hold your items and enough water to cover them, and that it is heatproof. And definitely be sure you place the container on a heatproof surface.

Mason/canning jars

These heatproof jars work very well in the sous vide bath. You can use them to pickle vegetables, make sauces or even prepare desserts. If you make any recipes that require Mason jars, you absolutely will also need canning tongs, which will help you add and remove jars from hot water safely.

Sous vide device

The many immersion circulators and sous vide bath machines on the market achieve the same results and the device you select is a matter of preference and type of sous vide task you need it for. The difference between the two styles (circulator or bath), however, is that the bath style is a stand-alone device that you can fill with water before adding your food item, whereas the circulator is a smaller device that can be attached to an external container of water. Water baths are slightly pricier, have a larger footprint in your kitchen and have a fixed internal capacity. A compact immersion circulator allows you to control the size of the water bath, which is especially helpful if you want to cook larger items that will not fit into the sous vide bath machine. The immersion circulator is also a much smaller machine and can be stored away in a kitchen cabinet or drawer when you are finished using it. There are a few quality brands

From left to right: Joule, Polyscience, Anova

available, with the most popular being PolyScience®, Anova™ and Joule®. The sous vide recipes prepared in this book were all cooked and tested with the PolyScience immersion circulator, which is my preference because it doubles as a professional and home cook device and has been a real soldier on very long cooks.

Vacuum bags or ziplock freezer bags

The second most important tool when cooking with your sous vide device is a collection of heatproof pouches in a variety of sizes. These bags are what separates your food from the heated water. You can use ziplock freezer bags if you do not own a vacuum sealer, by using the water displacement method (see page 11).

Vacuum sealer or chamber vacuum sealer

In sous vide, sealing foods in airtight bags is necessary for proper and even cooking. There is a difference between the two primary machines. Vacuum sealers such as FoodSaver® devices are great, especially for the home cook. They have a relatively small footprint and can be stored when not in use. The only limitation you have with this type of machine is in sealing liquids like soups and stews. These items cannot be properly vacuum-sealed without suctioning the liquid into the machine, which also can interfere with the plastic heat seal. Chamber-style vacuum sealers, on the other hand, are larger and relatively expensive, but they are more versatile and do an excellent job of quickly sealing or marinating foods. Additionally, the bags are available in different thickness options and can stand high heat over longer periods of time. The VacMaster® chamber sealer does an outstanding job of sealing liquids without making a mess, and you can freeze soups and stews flat in bags, which saves much needed freezer space. It all comes down to your personal preference and what sort of cooking you plan on doing. I use both a FoodSaver and a VacMaster depending on what my needs are. If you have neither of these tools, you will need to use ziplock freezer bags along with the water displacement method (see page 11). Just keep in mind that freezer bags cannot be used for very high temperatures or very long cooks.

Heatproof pouches separate your food from the heated water.

Vacuum sealers are necessary for even cooking.

acknowledgments

Writing this book would not have been possible without the help of some great people.

First, I would like to thank my editors, Elizabeth Seigle and Marissa Giambelluca; publisher Will Kiester; and the entire Page Street Publishing team for the opportunity to share my passion and food with the world.

I also would like to thank my best friend and partner, Emily Pihlquist, for keeping me motivated and believing in my ability to write this cookbook.

To some of the amazing people who have provided me with advice, contributions and insightful information for this book: V. Sheree Williams for writing such a thoughtful foreword, I am forever thankful; to the very talented food stylist/photographer team that worked very hard to bring my food from plate to page, Mandy Maxwell and Cheyenne Cohen, you two are amazing; Conor Bofin, Jennifer Booker, Shehu Fitzgerald, Eddie Gallagher, Sonia Mendez Garcia, Jesse Jones, Louise Leonard, Jim Masters, Elle Scott, Joy Stocke, Giada Valenti and Phil Wingo, your friendships are invaluable to me.

To my children, Lyasia and Justin, you both inspire me to always shoot for greatness. My siblings and immediate family members who always supported me, even in very tough times, I love y'all.

Big thanks to Chef Rachon Banks for dragging me out of the construction industry and into food service.

To all of the chefs and foodies who follow me on social media and my food blog, your loyalty and support helped make this happen, and you have my sincere gratitude!

about the author

Justice Stewart was raised in Ravenswood Houses in Queens, New York. He was a late-comer to the food industry, entering the culinary arena at age 40. He left a career in construction to pursue his passion of becoming a chef. In 2011 he started a food blog called Gourmet De-Constructed. He began his professional career as a cook servicing a major social media company. He went on to become a sous chef at Madison Square Garden cooking in a fine dining setting for the celebrity clientele during professional sporting events and concerts. He currently resides in Brooklyn, New York, with his girlfriend, Emily, and two cats, Kevin and Pablo.

index

aromatics, 11

arugula

Italian-Style Grilled Chicken Sandwich, 46

Sea Bass in Tuscan Kale, 119

asparagus

Butter and Garlic Asparagus, 155

Rack of Lamb with Butter and Garlic Asparagus, 94

avocado

Chacarero: Chilean Beef Sandwich, 22

Mexican Brunch Burger, 142

bacon: Crustless Quiche Lorraine, 145

bacteria, 11

Banana Pudding Pie with Rum-Infused Whipped Cream, 170

bath machines, 186–187

Béarnaise Sauce, 176

beef

See also veal

Argentine Skirt Steak with Chimichurri, 21

Beef Ramen, 34

Chacarero: Chilean Beef Sandwich, 22

Chateaubriand with Red Wine Sauce, 30

cooking times/temperatures, 12

Feijoada (Portuguese Stew), 69

Florentine Steak, 26

Guinness Corned Beef, 29

Gyro Sliders with Tzatziki, 124

Hawaiian Loco Moco, 146

Jamaican Oxtail Stew, 25

Memphis-Style Barbecue Bleu Cheese Burgers, 17

Mexican Brunch Burger, 142

Southeast Asian–Style Spicy Short Ribs, 33

Texas-Style Espresso-Rubbed Porterhouse, 18

bell peppers

Blackened Chicken Maque Choux, 45

Italian-Style Grilled Chicken Sandwich, 46

Mediterranean Octopus Salad, 107

Sausage and Peppers, 77

Sriracha-Glazed Duck with Pineapple Salsa, 65

Berry Cheesecake, 166

Beurre Blanc, 108

black beans: Feijoada (Portuguese Stew), 69

bleu cheese: Memphis-Style Barbecue Bleu Cheese Burgers, 17

botulism, 11

broiler, 185

browning meats, 185

burgers

Cumin-Spiced Lamb Burger, 89

Gyro Sliders with Tzatziki, 124

Hawaiian Loco Moco, 146

Memphis-Style Barbecue Bleu Cheese Burgers, 17

Mexican Brunch Burger, 142

butter, 11

cabbage

Cambodian-Style Chicken Salad, 58

Caramelized Cabbage Wedges, 156

canning jars, 11, 186

caramel sauce, 183

carrots

Buttery Root Vegetables, 159

Cambodian-Style Chicken Salad, 58

Honey-Glazed Heirloom Carrots, 151

cast-iron skillets, 185

chamber vacuum sealer, 187

Chateaubriand with Red Wine Sauce, 30

Cherry–Mustard Sauce, 74

chicken

Blackened Chicken Maque Choux, 45

Cambodian-Style Chicken Salad, 58

Chicken Shawarma with Pistachio Yogurt, 54

cooking times/temperatures, 12

Djaj Bil-Bahar Il-Asfar (Persian Spiced Chicken), 57

Garlicky Chicken Thighs, 49

Italian-Style Grilled Chicken Sandwich, 46

Madras Curry Chicken, 50

Spinach and Sundried Tomato–Stuffed Chicken Rolls, 53

chickpeas: Mediterranean Octopus Salad, 107

Chimichurri Sauce, 21

cooking racks, 186

cooking temperatures, 12–13

cooking times, 12–13

cooking vessels, 186

corn: Blackened Chicken Maque Choux, 45

couscous: Lamb Necks with Saffron Couscous, 90

crab

Crab Cakes with Poached Eggs and Saffron Hollandaise, 141

Veal Oscar, 37

Cracker Crust, 166

Crème Brûlée, Nutty, 169

cucumbers

Chicken Shawarma with Pistachio Yogurt, 54

Dill Pickles, 180

Mediterranean Octopus Salad, 107

Tzatziki, 124

desserts

Banana Pudding Pie with Rum-Infused Whipped Cream, 170

Berry Cheesecake, 166

Cardamom-Spiced Pears in Red Wine, 165

Nutty Crème Brûlée, 169

dried herbs, 11

duck

cooking times/temperatures, 12

Duck Leg Confit, 62

Pan-Seared Duck Breast with Pomegranate Dressing, 61

Sriracha-Glazed Duck with Pineapple Salsa, 65

Dulce de Leche, 183

eggs

Crab Cakes with Poached Eggs and Saffron Hollandaise, 141

Crustless Quiche Lorraine, 145

Hawaiian Loco Moco, 146

Mexican Brunch Burger, 142

equipment, 185–187

evaporation, 11

Farofa, 69

fish

See also seafood

cooking times/temperatures, 13

Dill Salmon, 111

Drunken Rose Red Snapper, 112

Monkfish with Saffron Beurre Blanc, 108

Pacific Salmon with Citrus Kale Salad, 104

Sea Bass in Tuscan Kale, 119

food safety, 11

FoodSaver®, 187

freezer bags, 11, 187

fruit

Berry Cheesecake, 166

Cardamom-Spiced Pears in Red Wine, 165

garlic

Butter and Garlic Asparagus, 155

Garlic Aioli, 89

Garlicky Chicken Thighs, 49

Garlic Mashed Potatoes, 160

Lamb Shanks with Garlic Mashed Potatoes, 98

green beans: Chacarero: Chilean Beef Sandwich, 22

green vegetables: cooking times/temperatures, 13

grills, 185

ham: Miami Cubano Sandwich, 73

heatproof cooking vessel, 186

heavy-bottom skillets, 185

herbs, 11

immersion circulators, 186–187

Juniper Butter, 38

kale

Pacific Salmon with Citrus Kale Salad, 104

Sea Bass in Tuscan Kale, 119

kitchen torch, 185

lamb

cooking times/temperatures, 12

Cumin-Spiced Lamb Burger, 89

Grilled Lamb Chops with Tomato–Prune Sauce, 97

Grilled Leg of Lamb with Gjetost Sauce, 93

Gyro Sliders with Tzatziki, 124

Lamb Necks with Saffron Couscous, 90

Lamb Shanks with Garlic Mashed Potatoes, 98

Moroccan-Style Sticky Meatballs, 123

Rack of Lamb with Butter and Garlic Asparagus, 94

lobster

Classic Lobster Rolls, 127

cooking times/temperatures, 13

Lobster Fettuccine in Herbed Cream Sauce, 103

low-temperature-long-time treatment (LTLT), 11

Madras Curry Powder, 50

Maillard reaction, 185

Mason jars, 11, 186

meatballs

Moroccan-Style Sticky Meatballs, 123

Sichuan Surf & Turf Meatballs, 131

microorganisms, 11

Monkfish with Saffron Beurre

Blanc, 108

mushrooms

Beef Ramen, 34

Hawaiian Loco Moco, 146

Pork Cutlets with Marsala Wine and Wild Mushrooms, 85

Sea Bass in Tuscan Kale, 119

noodles: Beef Ramen, 34

octopus

cooking times/temperatures, 13

Mediterranean Octopus Salad, 107

Pulpo Gallego, 132

olive oil, 11

onions: Pickled Red Onions, 179

Oxtail Stew, Jamaican, 25

oysters: Sichuan Surf & Turf Meatballs, 131

parsnips: Buttery Root Vegetables, 159

pasta: Lobster Fettuccine in Herbed Cream Sauce, 103

pasteurization, 11

Pastrami, Veal, 41

pears: Cardamom-Spiced Pears in Red Wine, 165

pickles

Dill Pickles, 180

Pickled Red Onions, 179

pie: Banana Pudding Pie with Rum-Infused Whipped Cream, 170

pineapple: Sriracha-Glazed Duck with Pineapple Salsa, 65

pistachios: Chicken Shawarma with Pistachio Yogurt, 54

pomegranate: Pan-Seared Duck Breast with Pomegranate Dressing, 61

pork

cooking times/temperatures, 12

Feijoada (Portuguese Stew), 69

Iberico Pork Tenderloin with Cherry–Mustard Sauce, 74

Lemongrass Pork Ribs, 81

Miami Cubano Sandwich, 73

Pernil, 70

Pork Cutlets with Marsala Wine and Wild Mushrooms, 85

"Roasted" Pork Belly, 82

Sausage and Peppers, 77

Sichuan Surf & Turf Meatballs, 131

Sweet and Spicy Soy-Glazed Pork Chops, 78

potatoes

Garlic Mashed Potatoes, 160

Lamb Shanks with Garlic Mashed Potatoes, 98

Pulpo Gallego, 132

Vinegar and Herb Potato Salad, 152

poultry

See also chicken; duck

cooking times/temperatures, 12

pudding: Banana Pudding Pie with Rum-Infused Whipped Cream, 170

Quiche Lorraine, Crustless, 145

Ramen, Beef, 34

raspberries: Berry Cheesecake, 166

Red Snapper, Drunken Rose, 112

ribs

Feijoada (Portuguese Stew), 69

Lemongrass Pork Ribs, 81

Southeast Asian–Style Spicy Short Ribs, 33

root vegetables

See also carrots; potatoes

Buttery Root Vegetables, 159

cooking times/temperatures, 13

rutabaga, Buttery Root Vegetables, 159

saffron
Lamb Necks with Saffron Couscous, 90
Saffron Hollandaise, 175
salads
Cambodian-Style Chicken Salad, 58
Mediterranean Octopus Salad, 107
Pacific Salmon with Citrus Kale Salad, 104
Vinegar and Herb Potato Salad, 152
salmon
Dill Salmon, 111
Pacific Salmon with Citrus Kale Salad, 104
sandwiches
See also burgers
Chacarero: Chilean Beef Sandwich, 22
Classic Lobster Rolls, 127
Italian-Style Grilled Chicken Sandwich, 46
Miami Cubano Sandwich, 73
sauces
Béarnaise Sauce, 176
Beurre Blanc, 108
Cherry–Mustard Sauce, 74
Chimichurri Sauce, 21
Dulce de Leche, 183
Gjetost Sauce, 93
Herbed Cream Sauce, 103
Lemongrass Sauce, 81
Red Wine Sauce, 30
Saffron Hollandaise, 175
Tomato–Prune Sauce, 97
sausages
Feijoada (Portuguese Stew), 69
Sausage and Peppers, 77
scallops
cooking times/temperatures, 13
Scallops à l'Américaine, 115
Scotch bonnet peppers, 25
Sea Bass in Tuscan Kale, 119

seafood
See also fish
Classic Lobster Rolls, 127
cooking times/temperatures, 13
Crab Cakes with Poached Eggs and Saffron Hollandaise, 141
Fiery Harissa, 135
Goan Shrimp, 116
Gochujang Cold Squid, 136
Lobster Fettuccine in Herbed Cream Sauce, 103
Mediterranean Octopus Salad, 107
Pulpo Gallego, 132
Scallops à l'Américaine, 115
seasoning blends
Goan Curry Paste, 116
Madras Curry Powder, 50
Spice Rub, 41
shrimp
cooking times/temperatures, 13
Fiery Harissa, 135
Goan Shrimp, 116
soups and stews
Beef Ramen, 34
Feijoada (Portuguese Stew), 69
sous vide
advantages of, 9
basics of, 11–13
devices, 186–187
equipment, 185–187
science of, 7
spinach
Italian-Style Grilled Chicken Sandwich, 46
Sea Bass in Tuscan Kale, 119
Spinach and Sundried Tomato–Stuffed Chicken Rolls, 53
Veal Roulades with Juniper Butter, 38
squid: Gochujang Cold Squid, 136

steak
Argentine Skirt Steak with Chimichurri, 21
Chacarero: Chilean Beef Sandwich, 22
Florentine Steak, 26
Texas-Style Espresso-Rubbed Porterhouse, 18
sundried tomatoes: Spinach and Sundried Tomato–Stuffed Chicken Rolls, 53

Tacos, Veal Tongue, 128
Tomato–Prune Sauce, 97
tools, 185–187
torch, 185
Tzatziki, 124

VacMaster®, 187
vacuum bags, 187
vacuum sealer, 187
veal
cooking times/temperatures, 12
Veal Oscar, 37
Veal Pastrami, 41
Veal Roulades with Juniper Butter, 38
Veal Tongue Tacos, 128
vegetables
See also specific vegetables
cooking times/temperatures, 13

water displacement method, 11
weights, 186

yogurt: Chicken Shawarma with Pistachio Yogurt, 54

ziplock bags, 11, 187